Smells of Childhood

Also available in this series:

Smells of Childhood

Memories of Small Heath

Mary M. Donoghue

ISIS
LARGE PRINT
Oxford, England

Copyright © Mary M. Donoghue 1997

First published in Great Britain 1997
by Brewin Books

Published in Large Print 1998 by ISIS Publishing Ltd,
7 Centremead, Osney Mead, Oxford OX2 0ES,
by arrangement with Brewin Books

British Library Cataloguing in Publication Data
Donoghue, Mary M.
  Smells of childhood. – Large print ed.
  1. Donoghue, Mary M. – Childhood and youth 2. Large type
  books 3. Great Britain – Biography
  I. Title
  941'.082'092

          ISBN 0-7531-5077-8

Printed and bound by MPG Books Ltd, Bodmin, Cornwall

I dedicate this book to my
late sister, Theresa.

With Love.

CONTENTS

ACKNOWLEDGMENTS

Thank You

1. Dr Carl Chinn — for your support, encouragement and faith in me, for which I shall always be very grateful. God Bless.
2. Linda, Terry, Jane and Gail — my children — I hope every Mother is as blessed with her children as I am with mine. My love for you all is eternal.
3. My Mother — for bringing the magic to my childhood. My love forever.
4. My late Father — for giving me the vision.
5. My brothers and sisters, for their memories and love, especially my late sister, Theresa, who always believed in me.
6. Dave Ruddick — Railtrack.
7. Colin Nash — Milepost 92$^1/_2$. (B.R. Photo Archives).
8. John Twort — Headmaster — Holy Family Primary School.
9. The headmaster and children of Holy Trinity School for giving me the opportunity to talk about the past.
10. Sandra Baty — Boots Fragrance counter.
11. Woolworth's Head Office.
12. Ann and John Thomson — for taking me "home".
13. Malcolm Allan — for the photographs of Small Heath.

14. Finally, my best friend, confidante, husband and lover — Gwyn. I have so much to thank you for darling, that the words would fill a million books. All my love, always. M.

FOREWORD

Carl Chinn

When Our Mom married Our Dad she left Aston Cross to live in Sparkhill. It was a big move, from the north side of the city over to the south, and there were many sights and sounds she missed about the old end. But it wasn't till after a few months that she put her finger, or rather her nose, on the one thing that really stood out between the two districts. 'Cus one, morning Our Mom woke up and realised that she could no longer smell the tangy HP Sauce, the hoppy Ansells Brewery and the pungent Nechells Gas Works.

Of course, Aston Cross wasn't the only part of Brum with its own distinctive aromas. Every one of our city's neighbourhoods was made special not only by its look and its clamour but also by the odours which wafted into the air. Over in Erdington it was the powerful whiff of rubber from Fort Dunlop, in Bournville it was the sickly-sweet taste of chocolate and cocoa drifting from Cadbury's, across the way in Tyseley it was the dampish trace of steam pushed out by the steam trains; and down by Montague Street, Bordesley, it was the reek of rubbish from the tip.

There's plenty more Brummagem places with a characteristic perfume and Mary Donoghue has made sure that scents of Small Heath will stand out amongst them, Vitally she has vividly captured all the senses of the neighbourhood in which she spent her childhood and youth.

With her leading us we go up its entries, mooch down its streets, traipse along its main roads and saunter through its parks and byeways. And all the while we see, feel, smell and hear the Small Heath of the past. Mary Donoghue has made sure that both Small Heath and its folk will not be forgotten.

PREFACE

Mary M. Donoghue

This book is about my early life in the mid-late 1950s to early 1960s and is based entirely on smells.

Small Heath had an abundance of smells, from the slaughterhouse at the rear of Bywaters butcher's shop, to the pungent, enticing "aroma" of the canal (or cut) in Garrison Lane.

Each chapter is, in effect, a mini-story depicting a young girl's thoughts and dreams and the reality of that time in her life.

My parents were Irish and came here, after my Father's sojourn in the RAF, with my two older brothers. For this reason I have started the book with a prologue about their meeting and finished it with an epilogue about my visit to Ireland in 1994.

CHAPTER
ONE

Childhood

Childhood
slips by,
almost without
notice,
unless we are
lucky enough
to be
blessed
with things that
make it
memorable —
I was very
lucky.

What is a Mother?

She's the one we turn to
when we feel lost and sad,
she's our steadying anchor,
the best friend we've ever had.
She's the one who went without
to keep us clothed and fed,
the one who dried our tears,
and tucked us up in bed.

She's the one who understood
our childhood hopes, and fears,
the one who praised our efforts
through all our growing years.
Her's the ever-helping hand,
freely given, not wanting gain,
the sympathetic, caring heart
when we have suffered pain.

She knows, some day, we'll leave her
as a new Life calls us on,
she'll smile as we go away,
yet will cry when we are gone.
Her love stays warm within us,
for she has been our Star
who loved, cared, and cherished us,
and made us what we are.

THIS is a Mother.

Inheritance
Dublin 8.12.1941

"Do you, Jane Margaret, take William Joseph Kiernan . . ."

Jane, although always called Jean by all who knew her, 21 years old, pretty and shy, her smart grey two-piece suit resurrected from more affluent times, small pillbox hat not quite covering her auburn curls, smart grey court shoes pinching her toes, stood nervously at the altar.

Bill, 32, slim figure handsome in his uniform, stood confidently at her side. After a two year courtship these two people, from differing backgrounds, were about to become one.

Jean, convent-school educated, had lived all her life in the city of Dublin, a true city girl, and totally at ease with the noise and bustle all around her. Her job with Mr Fuscoe, a fiery Italian, in the local tobacconist/confectioner's shop, kept her in touch with the daily happenings in her community and she shared in the joys and sorrows of the people. The youngest of five children, having two sisters and two brothers, both of the latter had sadly died when only in their late twenties, she still managed to enjoy her life. Blessed with the voice of an angel, having sung at the Queens Theatre Dublin and the British and Irish Steam Packet Company where her Father worked, her world had widened with the appearance of Bill on a winter day in 1939.

Bill, eldest of five children, having one sister and three brothers, had been brought up deep in the heart of a small village in County Wexford, in the small two bed-roomed cottage that his great-great grandfather had built with his bare hands. Before joining the Forces he had travelled the length and breadth of Ireland, going wher-ever his fancy, and his bicycle, took him.

Bill lived by his wits and his clever hands, collecting potatoes, gathering the crops, doing myriad jobs for various farmers across the West of Ireland. He mended shoes with a dexterity unknown to the best of cobblers, and his sewing was neater than any tailor. He was a crack shot, shooting game with an accuracy envied by all, a fountain of knowledge stored in his clever brain. Yet he was a quiet man, content with himself He fished the mighty Shannon with a piece of string and a twig, then cooked his catch in a lonely field under the light of the stars. He had a countryman's ways, was soft spoken and a great one for the "crack".

He once told me that he had fallen in love with Jean when she was just 14 years old and singing in Phoenix Park in the summer of 1934. It was to be five long years before he met the owner of the voice he fell in love with that day. She had arrived at the Dublin Barracks to collect medicine for her sick soldier brother-in-law, lost and confused. Bill had kindly shown her the way to the pharmacy and had looked after her ever since. Despite the eleven year age gap they were suited, my Mother's gaiety balanced by my Father's seriousness.

I can imagine the shock to my Mother's system on arriving in war-torn Britain in 1945. My Father had already seen the devastation during his sojourn in the RAF. Birmingham had received more than its fair share of damage and my Mother often told me how upset she was at the sights she beheld; hundreds of bombed sites, children running round crying, yet the people of Birmingham simply picked themselves up and got on with their lives.

Housing was very scarce and, to my parents' dismay, no lodging house would take them in with my two brothers who were only two and three at that time. Forced to place the boys in a children's home, my parents sought frantically for a place to live where they could be a family again.

After many months they were finally housed in what was grandly termed a "two up, two down, back to back", one of a set of four houses in a yard in Small Heath. They were told it was to be "temporary" accommodation which, in their case, lasted for sixteen years!

Mother told of how hard it was for my Father to find work, of the never-ending battle against dirt and creepy-crawlies and food rationing. Somehow they managed and began to make a home for their little family.

During the next sixteen years four more children were born into the family, all girls, but I remember my Mother giving birth to a still-born baby boy when I was just thirteen, and how devastated we all were.

Mother loved the cinema, and quite often we children would have an enforced afternoon off school so we could accompany her. We didn't really mind as we too loved the cinema. She made lovely soda bread, curly-kale (dark green cabbage and mashed potatoes) and lots of dishes peculiar to her home, which we tried to emulate as we grew up, but without success. She gave

5

me the gift of laughter and the joy of living. My Father loved the outdoors and on sunny summer days I would cycle alongside him to the countryside, exploring until hunger and tiredness drove us home. He taught me many things on those outings, not only the names of trees and flowers, but how to relax and be at peace with myself. Our childhood was filled with the songs my Mother sang, "Danny Boy", "Kathleen" etc. Every fortnight I would collect our copy of Ireland's Own from the local newsagents, eager to get home so we could all devour the song sheets in the centre. My Father would choose his favourites and Mother would sing, to the one-finger efforts on the old piano by my brother Jim. Sometimes, when Father had had a pint or two, he would join in and our house would ring with sound.

On dark winter evenings they regaled us with stories of their childhood and courtship, their different life-styles, of the little people, the ghosts and the Banshee. We would creep into bed praying that nothing would harm us that night, and to make extra sure would touch the feet of the Crucifix on the bedroom wall.

Father often said he would "one day" take me to Ireland as I was enthralled by his tales. His eyes would grow misty as he spoke of the beautiful mountains, the River Shannon and the warmth of the people. I never envisaged my Mother being with us on our journey, perhaps because all her family had moved to England after the war, and it was easy to visit them. I often wondered if my Father missed his old life but he never did tell me. From the moment I started work I prayed for the day when we would go on our travels together, but

6

money was very scarce and the promised trip never took place.

My Mother is now in her 77th year and is still beautiful and the life and soul of every gathering. Sadly my Father died seventeen years ago, but will remain in my heart forever.

The stories they told us are part of the family tapestry and have built up a far better picture than any photograph could ever capture. My love and thanks for being their daughter cannot be measured, not least because it is from them stems my love of the Emerald Isle and its people.

CHAPTER
TWO

Everywhere

On special days
I take out
my childhood memories,
and wrap them round me, like a cloak,
for my Life was made from these:

In the bustle of
the old Cov Road,
the splendour of the Grange,
its heroes and heroines
making me feel strange.

In dark corners of
the pawn shop,
in Gittens second-hand domain,
in Maud's gas-lit emporium,
and "Raggy Allen's" down the lane.

Green Lane baths
swallowed my fears
in its ozone-laden pool,

the library knew my ambitions
when I was leaving school.

Our Church held
all my secrets
in its smoky, incensed air,
wrapped in every statue,
in every wooden chair.

Yes, everywhere
in Old Small Heath
I left my childish dreams,
caught in the ashes of the bombed sites
and the taste of
Walls ice creams.

The Yard

Little Green Lane, Small Heath, was long and narrow, containing various styles of houses and shops. I often wondered why it was called a lane, so totally bereft of trees and grass it bore little resemblance to any lane I'd seen in books. Mrs H, our next door neighbour, always referred to it as the "Horse Road"; the only horse I ever saw was the rag and bone man's old nag.

In this hotch-potch of architecture dwelt people from many different walks of life, and countries. There were quite a few Irish families, ourselves included, as well as Indians, Scottish and Welsh, all living in perfect harmony. The wonderful thing was that everyone looked out for one another, going so far as to loan someone a pair of "best" sheets whenever a visit from the doctor was imminent. I think Mrs H had loaned her sheets out to most of the families in our yard in those days.

The yard held four houses, two on the left hand side with a small brewhouse at one end of the second house, and two at the top end of the yard, the walls of number four (our house) resting against the partly-demolished wall of the yard next door and a bombed site. Around the corner from Mrs H's house, were the two toilets for the use of the occupants of all four houses. In reality we only had the use of one as Mrs H, having been the first occupant of the yard some years before, had sole use of the second one. A padlock on the door kept everyone out, until my brother Jim found out how to pick the lock. We gaped in astonishment when he did, not for Mrs H's family the bare blue brick floor, discoloured walls, strips of daily newspapers hanging on a rusty nail behind the door, and a metal chain without a handle.

The floor was covered in wood-effect lino, effectively hiding its bareness, together with a neat, fluffy blue mat around the base of the loo. A bicycle lamp hung strategically from the cold water pipe which, when switched on, cast its yellow glow over the whitewashed walls. Proper toilet paper, pristine white, hung from a small white plastic holder on the wall to the right hand side of the loo, and a round metal ball swung gently from the base of the chain. Best of all was the fragrance of clean fresh pine, conjuring up images of forests in far off lands, permeating the small room. Peering into the bowl of the loo we saw the tiny square green block which created the scent. I am ashamed to admit that I actually pinched a couple of sheets of the toilet paper, hastily pushing it up my cardigan sleeve lest Mr or Mrs H suddenly appear, which I kept in a small box under my bed, along with my other "treasures" until, eventually, it simply disintegrated into a ragged ball of pine-scented paper. It wasn't worth the shame I felt when I had to confess to Father O'Keefe the following Saturday, espe-cially when he advised me it was stealing! I promised my God I wouldn't use it, just hang on to it for a keepsake. Well I couldn't really put it back could I!

Our Jim spent a whole day in our loo once, he'd pinched what he thought was half a bar of chocolate which was lying on the kitchen shelf. It turned out to be Ex-lax (a laxative) — Mother agreed with us that it served him right for taking something that wasn't his. I often wondered if he confessed!

11

The brew-house contained a huge metal boiler and a mottled yellow stone sink. I never knew why it was called a brew house for no beers were ever brewed in there, to my knowledge anyway. Every Monday, whatever the weather, most of the women in the back houses could be seen boiling, scrubbing and rinsing their washing, then pushing it through the huge rollers of an enormous green mangle before hanging it in long, stately rows on the thick rope washing lines strung along the length of the yard. I loved the smell on washing days, Persil soap powder, Lifebuoy scrubbing soap, bleach, Robin's starch and Jeyes Fluid, the latter being used to scour out the sink and boiler when the washing was finally hung out to dry. Home-made props, which were always collapsing under the weight, vainly struggled to support the loads. Many times I ran through the lines of washing, rubbing my face in the cavalry twill sheets so I could inhale their essence, until a clip round the ear sent me scurrying home!

Each time I passed the burgundy and cream exterior, always reminding me of strawberry and vanilla ice-cream, of the Court Steam Laundry at Bordesley Green those self-same smells drifted out on the air, reminding me of the yard.

The yard had its own special smell which came from the centre drain, which in summer was caked with dried mud (which came from Heaven knows where), sending a sharp, musty smell into the air. In winter the drain often over-flowed and the murky-grey water, lapping around our feet as we played, emitted a not unpleasant, though sharp, moist scent throughout the yard.

An air-raid shelter dominated the yard, its high brick walls, metal doors and glistening concrete roof, the latter embedded with what looked like bits of glass, casting dark shadows over the rest of the yard. It stood squarely in front of our small kitchen window, thus minimising the light, forcing us to use the gas-light throughout the days of winter and summer.

The interior was awash with all kinds of rubbish; mattresses, prams, bedsteads, broken chairs, in fact all kinds of things and the smell was even more pungent than the centre drain. To me it smelled like all the things I hated — cockroaches, bugs and mice. All these creatures, and anything else that fancied a nice warm home, found its way into that shelter. Needless to say the girls kept well away from it, except when we used its stout walls as a blackboard when playing "schools". The boys braved the unknown every October, only too willing to disgorge its contents onto the blue cobbled bricks of the yard in their search for anything which would burn on our annual bonfire.

The days before Bonfire Night were exciting. Every evening, weather permitting, Mother would allow us to trundle the home-made cart up to the corner of Coventry Road and Green Lane in order to collect pennies for the Guy. The public didn't realise that our Guy was real as I used one of the children, who lived in one of the front houses, for this purpose. We'd black his face with soot from the barrow and caution him to keep as still as possible, telling him he wouldn't have any "sweetie" money if he moved so much as a muscle! On one such evening an elderly gentleman touched our Guy's face, recoiling with shock when it laughed! Unfortunately our real-live Guy was short-lived when his Mother came home early one evening and saw us trying to brush the soot off his clothes!

Our prewar (I often wondered which war!), two-up, one down and a scullery, tried in vain to stretch itself as our family increased with rapid regularity. The bombed site in the next yard prevented it from going anywhere, and groaning and heaving it would settle into whatever shape the shifting cobbles decreed.

A delicate gas mantle, the only source of light in our small square living room, often flickered and died, usually when Mother hadn't any more money, the gossamer flakes drifting down on to whatever meal we were enjoying at the time. Then we would sit by the light of the fire and the naked, hissing flame from the, now bare, gas pipe, listening to stories of long ago. My Mother was a wonderful story-teller then, and in the gloom of that room it was easy to imagine the scenes of her childhood. We often wondered why we hadn't electricity, the only house in the yard not to be so endowed. Mother said it was because the accommodation was only temporary.

The scullery and bedrooms never had gas mantles as these were one old penny each, so were an expensive commodity as they didn't last very long. Naked flames roared to the ceiling in those rooms, leaving circles of dark brown stains on the distempered surfaces.

On entering other houses in the yard I was overcome by the brightness created by electric bulbs and small lamps, the lovely wallpaper, even on the bedroom walls, and the smart rag rugs in front of modern tiled fireplaces.

Most of the families had television sets and gramo-phones, the latter usually concealed within dark, wooden cabinets. Mrs H even had an electric radio which matched her gramophone! I felt then we missed out on a lot of pleasure because of the lack of electricity. Going back inside our own, dark house was like stepping back in time.

A huge cast-iron black range took up most of one wall of our living room, the job of black-leading this fell to me when I was old enough. Its huge ovens on either side of the fire had many uses. Not only did Mother put our clothes in there to air, she also produced the most delicious apple pies in minutes. Over the open part of the fire was a long, black protruding arm holding a huge saucepan. When money was in short supply Mother would place all the ingredients for Irish stew in this pan, its spicy smell emanating throughout the house and the yard and, on occasion when she put mutton in, right out into the lane itself.

An old piano rested against yet another wall, shuffling for space with the chiffonier, this was a sort of huge sideboard with mirrors, which took up more space than any other piece of furniture in the room. A small settee sat underneath the plate glass window, facing the scrubbed wooden table which was the centre-piece of the room. Against the table rested odd chairs, some made by my Father, their scarred and bent legs evidence of the ill-treatment they received when we played musical chairs to the strains of Mario Lanza played on the old wind-up gramophone. The whole room smelled

15

of lavender polish in the summer and mutton stew in winter.

Our scullery contained the coal-house, which was really just an alcove at the side of the stairs, where we stored our fuel during the winter. In summer Mother draped a floral curtain over the gap to hide its empty ugliness.

Just to the right of the kitchen door was the gas stove, its grey and white mottled surface a never-ending source of frustration for Mother. No matter how often she scrubbed it, it never seemed to look really clean. Along the exterior wall was the sink of deep yellow stone, its cavernous interior slightly pink through constant scrubbing with bleach, the cold water tap slightly askew, the results of my Father turning it too fiercely one day.

A small wooden draining board, worn smooth at the edges, ran to the left of the sink, its pale brown surface pitted and scarred. Just at head-height was a linoleum covered shelf, holding my Father's shaving mug, brush and razor. A small, single-paned window behind the shelf fought bravely to bring light into the room, but was defeated by the bulk of the air-raid shelter. At one end of the shelf Mother stored her cleaning materials, which was almost our Jim's undoing. He adored milk and came in from school one day, grabbed a milk bottle from the end of the shelf, which unknown to him held Jeyes Fluid which, when diluted, closely resembles milk, and took a huge swallow. Tears poured down his face as, choking, he dropped the bottle on the floor. Fortunately Mother was on hand to pour pints of salt water down his throat, so avoiding any permanent damage. His breath smelt funny for ages afterwards.

Bath nights were a constant source of embarrassment as far as I was concerned. As the water had to be heated in the saucepan on the fire as well as other saucepans on the stove, it was never changed. By the time I stepped in the water was luke-warm, due to our being bathed in descending age order. The bath, which hung on the kitchen wall Monday to Friday, had been repaired many times by my Father. The small, round metal washers he used would, eventually, turn rusty, the water taking on a dingy-brown hue which, thankfully, never stained our skin. These washers were quite sharp if we happened to sit on them! I loved it when Mother bought a bar of Camay soap instead of the usual Lifebuoy scrubbing variety!

After washing our hair in Derbac shampoo "just in case", the smell of which I hated, Mother dried our hair with a rough towel, then dragged a steel comb through the tangles she created. I think this is one of the reasons my brothers started losing their hair at an early age! I loved it when she tried our hair in different styles, putting rags around our tresses, or even dinky curlers, after which she'd pat Amami setting lotion on the hidden curls, the smell of which lingered in our hair for days.

Despite the difference in our religious beliefs and lifestyles everyone in the yard got on well, it was like being part of one big happy family. We had something very precious in that yard: people who cared.

CHAPTER
THREE

Mixed-Up

Sugar and tea,
biscuits galore,
boxes and tins
piled up on the floor.

Crumbly corned beef,
and jellied ham
under a glass shelf,
next to the spam.

Bundles of firewood,
bags of "Coalite"
nestle together
in the dim light.

Bacon and sausage,
butter and cheese,
such wonderful scents
our taste buds to tease.

Maud's big black cat
sniffed avidly

at every item
she gave to me.

With a kind word,
a nice little smile
Maud made shopping
less of a toil.

"Maud" and Others

Maud would smile as I pushed the grimy list into her outstretched hands. I can still see Mother's scrawled . . . "I'd be obliged if you'd let me have 1lb sugar, $1/2$lb Echo . . ." and then, right at the bottom, almost as if Mother didn't want Maud to see it ". . . and 10 Players Weights".

Carefully Maud placed each item on the scrubbed, lino-covered counter top, watched by her black and white tom cat who lay sprawled at the side of the bacon slicer. The cat's lazy tail swished backwards and forwards in tune with the hiss of the wicked blades, and occasionally flicking at a fly who'd been fortunate in escaping the fate of its kind on the long, thickly-studded fly-paper which hung from the ceiling, finishing level with Maud's eyebrows. I don't know how that cat never lost part of his tail, but am sure he must have come dangerously close over the years.

Everyone in Little Green Lane and the surrounding streets frequented Maud's little shop. It sold everything from firewood at twopence a bundle to hot, crusty bread and "slightly" salty bacon. We queued in there most days from Monday to Friday, always with a list of things "on tick" and then go in, heads held high, on Friday nights to pay for our week's sustenance. The circle never really closed, we'd pay for everything on Friday and start having things on credit again on Saturday morning!

Maud was an amazing woman for I never once saw her write down the cost of anything we purchased there but, come Friday night, she knew to the exact penny how much was owing to her. She had no calculator or new fangled till in those days, just her clever brain.

I adored the smells that lingered in that shop, whether they came from Maud herself, she of the well-scrubbed, shiny face, flowered "pinny" draped around her slim figure, large red hands, with wisps of black hair jutting out from the tartan turban she wound round her head, or was just a glorious mixture of Lifebuoy scrubbing soap, Jeyes Fluid, soda crystals and the pungent aroma of the various cheeses, I don't know. I loved it because it smelled so clean.

The interior of the shop was a hotch-potch of commodities, all jostling for space on the crowded shelves, under the counter and in the glass display case. I was always amazed at the variety of the goods she sold, and how three or four women at a time could cram into the small amount of floor space in front of the counter! At Christmas time her shop was filled to overflowing as even more goods arrived, along with longer queues of people. Never appearing to be flustered, she coped with them all, with a smile and a kind word. I can see her now, standing, hands on hips, as she listened patiently to her customers moans, groans or good news, nodding or shaking her head in the appropriate places.

I must have been about eleven the first time Mother asked me to go and collect the "chocolates". When I made my request Maud disappeared underneath the counter and re-appeared with a newspaper wrapped parcel. As mother had a very sweet tooth and a penchant for Bluebird toffees and Fillery's caramels (Mother always called them "carmels"!) I didn't think anything of her buying a whole box of chocolates. As soon as I got home Mother grabbed the package from me and dashed upstairs.

Mystified, but too well brought up to pry, I just assumed Mother would share them out later when Father had gone to his Whist Drive. All evening I waited for them to be handed round, my taste buds drooling in anticipation, but I was sadly disappointed. I lay in bed that night thinking how greedy Mother was as she obviously ate the chocolates whilst we were in bed. It was many years before I knew the real contents of what she really wanted, sanitary towels, so she and Maud had come up with the unlikely code-name!

Mrs E's shop was totally different to Maud's. It didn't feel as cosy and welcoming somehow, maybe because Mrs E and Maud were totally different in every way. She was small and round, her laughter-lined face slightly tanned, as if she'd spent her life in the sun. The shelves in her shop weren't filled to bursting, instead selected items such as Bournville Cocoa, Heinz baked beans, Robinsons marmalade, golden and sweet, sat majestically on clean white-papered shelves, their very austerity daring anyone to touch them.

Sometimes Mrs E's eldest son served in the shop and we girls loved him! He was very tall, with dark wavy hair, his features very much like his mother but his manner very aloof. I think he went to Grammar School, which put him out of our reach anyway. I was really glad Mrs E didn't allow credit — a large notice confirming this took pride of place on the rear, white-painted wall of the shop — for I couldn't have looked her son in the face again if I'd had to hand him one of Mother's scribbled, mis-spelt requests. For some reason Mother always got her "P's" and "B's" mixed up, a quirk Maud was used to, and laughing called out, providing no-one else was in the shop, "one tin of peans, two tins of bees" but without malice.

Mingled with the scent of the Brylcreem Mr E Junior put on his hair was the delicious smell of spicy foods wafting through from the living quarters of the shop. We knew, just by the smell, that we had never tasted anything like it, but that the E family were fond of it was perfectly obvious. Small tins of curry powder, chilli and other spices adorned a small space to one side of a shelf nearest the door to the family abode. I never saw any of the local people purchasing these items so could only assume they were for the sole use of the family. When I had my first curry, at the age of nineteen, the delicious aroma took me back in time to Mrs E's shop.

I don't ever remember meeting Mr E, except as a flying figure in a grey raincoat dashing along the lane early each weekday morning. My Mother said she thought he was "in business". Strangely I never saw Maud's husband either, only as a shadowy figure espied through the opaque glass of the door connecting the living room to the shop. In those days, or so it seemed, the women looked after the men, whatever their station in life.

The scents that filled the air in those two shops had certainly never reached the slaughterhouse! Quite often, after school, Jim dragged me, protesting quite loudly, along to the rear of Bywaters, the butchers on the Coventry Road. Stealthily we made our way around to

23

the yard to stand at the huge open doorway of the slaughterhouse. Here giant-sized men, with glistening muscles, wielded large, scythe-like knives with which to slit the pigs' throats, after first stunning them with a kind of electric tong.

I watched, in fascinated horror, as the soft pink flesh, which rapidly turned white, sprang open and the warm blood gushed into the trough-like drain set in the floor. I have never been able to forget the squeals of those animals, nor the smell. In Summer the air was thick with the mingled stench of warm, fresh blood and something else I was never able to define as a child — in retrospect I believe it was fear. From then until now I have never eaten pork products for as soon as I enter a butcher's shop the putrid smells come back to haunt me.

The Wool Shop, next door to Mrs E's, was run by a lovely lady called Jane. She was quite rounded, fluffy blonde hair surrounding a rosy-cheeked face, her full lips always curved into a smile of welcome. Her whole manner was relaxed, as if she hadn't a care in the world. I spent a lot of time there, just lounging around, pretending to look at the various patterns, whilst she served her real customers.

Brightly coloured garments, hats and mittens, all knitted or crocheted by Jane, adorned the plain yellowing walls, and I longed to be able to reproduce just one of them, but never did. Sometimes she'd display goods in the window that her customers made, often selling them so she and the customer would be more than happy.

Most of the women bought very little in the way of

goods, but Jane didn't seem to mind and enjoyed the gossip that abounded. With a cup of tea, in a white china cup, held in her be-ringed hands, she was quite content to sit on her stool, head tilted to one side as she listened to the gossip.

Hand-knitted mohair cardigans, of varying shades from purest white (her summer wear) through all the colours of the rainbow to a beautiful deep shade of purple at Christmas time, covered her ample frame. These always had some kind of silvery motif attached to either a shoulder or lapel, which glittered and shimmered as her bosom shook with laughter, or shivered with tears, depending on the story she was listening to at the time.

On reflection I don't ever recall seeing Jane's legs, mainly because her cardigans covered her from neck to below waist level as she sat on her stool. No matter what time of day we visited the shop she was always sitting on that stool and Mother thought she may have had something wrong with her legs, but we never did find out.

Whenever Mother was expecting a "happy" event, Jane sorted out the easiest patterns for me to attempt, stretching from her stool to the shelves underneath the counter. She once tried to guide me through the intricacies of crochet, but gave up when she saw the tangled mess I produced.

My eldest brother, Denis, taught me to knit one very hot summer day. I had purchased a ball of rainbow coloured wool and a pair of blue plastic needles, total cost 1/6d (less than eight new pence), being the sum total

25

of money collected from the men whose cars I'd minded the previous Saturday.

Side by side, we sat on Mrs E's doorstep whilst he showed me how to cast on, never losing his temper when I got it wrong. We received many strange looks from the other children, especially the boys, but Denis ignored the jibes, not an easy task for a boy of nearly fifteen, and who was looked up to by the younger boys. With his help I managed to produce a fairly reasonable pair of bootees, one slightly larger than the other, and knitted in plain stitch as Denis didn't know how to do purl, but they were knitted with love. I felt really proud when Mother put them on Jean the very first time she took her out in the pram!

Jane's shop had a warm, caressing feel which wrapped itself around all who shopped there. The crisp, new paper patterns smelled of ink and I loved the aroma, even though the print sometimes came off on my fingers when I was knitting, transforming whatever colour wool I was using into a grubby mess!

After Jane left the shop, we never found out why, it was taken over by a lady who was a lot older than Jane and who didn't really like the children browsing around.

The tobacconist juggled for space on the slight curve in the lane, facing onto Arsenal Street. The tall, thin houses on either side had tried for many years to push the shop out of existence but had failed. Its two high, worn steps bore the marks of many feet, a permanent groove in the lower step a legacy of the past. Pipes, of varying shapes and sizes, filled the glass-fronted shelves. Packets of tobacco and pipe cleaners lay under gleaming glass covers alongside packets of cigars from exotic sounding places. Sometimes I purchased Father's cigarettes from here, usually if Maud had run out of his particular brand (a very rare occurrence indeed). I lingered as long as possible, allowing other customers to be served first, just so I could inhale the smell.

A piece of dark red, highly polished leather sat squarely on the dark wooden counter top, and with fascination I watched as Mr N unrolled a pouch of tobacco, for the more affluent customers, on its surface. With a long, silver-coloured spoon he carefully placed flakes of this fragrant smelling substance on the brass weighing scales, look at the customer who would either nod or shake his head, before placing the flakes into parchment-like paper which, with a flick of his wrist, he twisted into a cone shape before handing it over.

Like Mrs E's shop, the smells conjured up far off places and I longed to be grown up so I could, one day, visit some of them. Cuba, China, India — my imagination ran riot as I tried to absorb all the different odours at once. It was like stepping into another world, one of luxury and finesse, from the green-shaded bulb hanging from the centre of the ceiling, the dust free goods behind their protective glass, the well-groomed appearance of Mr N's elderly frame to the dark red polished linoleum on the floor.

Mr N strutted proudly around his shop, grey suited body erect, head high on his shoulders. A pristine white shirt, with matching starched collar, gleamed whitely beneath the maroon and silver waistcoat he wore under the suit. A silver watch-chain stretched across his chest

27

and I loved to see him withdraw the watch from his tiny waistcoat pocket, put it to his ear, shake it and then return it to its dark home, without even looking at the time! I once asked my Father if he'd like a pocket watch and chain, to which he replied he didn't need one for couldn't he tell the time by the light of the sun!

Wheelers, the greengrocers, was on the corner of little Green Lane and Arsenal Street, its buckets of "ready-peeled" potatoes placed in the coolest part of the shop, the water in which they wallowed emitting a strange, pungent smell, and which were never purchased by my Mother. Her reason for this was, as she put it, "Sure, don't they take away half the spud when they peel them!" As we used at least six pounds of potatoes at every meal I can understand her concern.

Serried rows of apples, oranges, pomegranates and lemons, their scents well known to us, their taste denied, lay along shelves against the rear wall of the shop. These fruits always attracted wasps, so I stayed well away from them, usually ordering my goods from the safety of the open doorway so I could run away if a wasp appeared. Mr Wheeler, his round stomach covered by a white, three-quarter length jacket, the middle buttons always on the verge of parting company with the buttonholes, smiled, his blue eyes twinkling behind the gold-rimmed spectacles as he weighed the produce.

Mrs Wheeler seemed to spend her days polishing all the fruit with a soft white cloth, the rosy red of the apples making me think of the wicked stepmother in Snow White and the Seven Dwarfs. Her fluffy blonde curls bounced merrily on her shoulders as her strong arms wielded the cloth, almost as if she was attacking something. Her ample bosom heaved with the effort, and a blush often suffused me when I espied the male populace staring at her, praying to my God that I would never be encumbered by such a chest! In this instance my prayers were answered!

Flowers of all descriptions stood in vases, urns, buckets and basins, their sweet, sometimes cloying, smells masking the earthy aroma of many-eyed King Edward potatoes. New-laid eggs, at just one penny each, rested, pointed end up, in grey cardboard trays by the side of the till. They gleamed and I often thought Mrs Wheeler must have polished them as well as everything else. The whole shop smelled of fresh air and sunshine, even in Winter, and I can still recall the thrill I felt as I stood in the ever-open doorway, quite willing to let other customers be served first, inhaling the delightful scents to my heart's content. I think I would have enjoyed working for a greengrocer if it wasn't for the wasps!

When I visit the supermarkets now, with their "multiple choice" products, the never-ending queues at the check-outs, no human contact and totally bereft of any kind of smell, I feel sad that my children and grandchildren will never know what a joy shopping can be.

CHAPTER
FOUR

Hand-Me-Downs

Shoes,
coats,
dresses,
hats,
all
bought
for
sixpence — if that!

Suits,
blouses,
jumpers
too,
but
all
second-hand,
making me blue.

Second-Hand

I dreaded the shout of "Any old rags?", because I knew Mother would send me out to the rag and bone man with a bundle of old dusters, most of which were her worn-out bloomers! These were knickers which ended just above the knee, and for some strange reason best known to the manufacturers, were only ever two colours, blue or pink.

The old man who collected the rags, we never knew his name or where exactly he came from, his weary horse feeling the weight of the over-loaded cart with plastic bags of suffering goldfish hanging from the sides, fingered the bundles, his dirty hands almost caressing the fabric. His grey, lined face, bloodshot eyes squinting in response to the smoke curling round his face from the hand-rolled cigarette he kept permanently in the corner of his mouth, broke into a grin as he hissed "Twopence or a goldfish?", his hands already reaching into garments, not much better than those piled on the cart, for the coins he knew I'd take. Just once I longed to be able to ask for a goldfish instead, not just to see the surprise on his face, but also to rescue at least one of those beleaguered fish!

The smell which emanated from the cart was horrible, and I often wondered what some of the items had been used for! Mother's bundles always smelled of Lavender polish or bleach, and the old man sneezed each time he took my offerings, sending his horse into nervous jerks, resulting in him leaving a "deposit" on the road, which some of the children quickly scooped up, having waited especially for this moment! With snarls and shouts the old man tried to chase them off, but they had got this particular task down to a fine art. Laughing and jeering they ran off up the lane, to sell their illegal gains to those fortunate enough to have gardens. Much as I liked the idea of having some money I wasn't prepared to soil my hands, or insult my nostrils, with the smell of manure!

"Raggy Allen's", a huge building on Garrison Lane, was where everyone took their old clothes in exchange for cash. I'm sure Raggy's must have been the first place where we heard the term "re-cycling".

Our Theresa thought it had something to do with bicycles! Far too often, as far as I was concerned, I scurried down the lane, youngest sister's dolls' pram piled high with old clothes, to sell at Raggy's. Each type of fabric was weighed separately as the price was different for each one, and I would cringe with embarrassment when the young man (why were they always young?) held up some of the more "delicate" garments, saying "What kind of fabric is this then, love?", a cheeky grin on his face. Everyone, at some time, procured cash for their cast-off clothing, which never ceased to amaze me as most of them had been purchased from jumble sales or the second-hand shops! A stale, sweaty sort of smell hung in the air, in and around the building, making me feel claustrophobic, worsening in Summer as the smells jostled for supremacy over that of the canal just along the lane! I prayed to my God to let me be an adult as soon as possible so I wouldn't then have to patronise Raggy Allen's!

The pawn shop, its three brass balls highly polished,

lurked in an alleyway, opposite the Wrexham public house and to one side of the slaughterhouse, its front windows brightly lit, proud to display the rich goods on offer, unredeemed pledges, but the rear shop held only one dingy bulb, strewn with fly-paper and cobwebs. A bright light would have seemed alien in there, where people pawned (hocked as it was called then) anything they could to tide them over until pay-day.

Some of the items had been taken there so often it was like a second home to them, I'm sure! Father's "best" tweed jacket, purchased from a jumble sale, and painstakingly repaired by him until it looked almost brand new, its soft leather elbow-pieces smelling of the oil he used to prevent them from creaking, only resided there occasionally as he needed it once every week to wear to the Whist Drives he so enjoyed.

Wedding rings spent more time in the dark recesses of the pawn shop than they ever did on the owner's finger! Each time I took Mother's in I cringed as the clerk, who was as dry and worn as the room in which he earned his daily bread, held it up to the light. With eyebrows drawn together in a frown, the ash from the cigarette in the corner of his mouth falling, unseen, on to nicotine-stained fingers, face creased with concentration, he'd cough "How much was she expecting for this, then?", his tone derogatory. From somewhere I found the courage to answer with dignity, "The usual ten shillings please, Sir!", always overly polite in case he reduced the amount.

Everywhere reeked of stale cigarettes, dust, decay, and when the street door opened a whiff of the dreadful stench of the slaughterhouse invaded the room. The yellowing walls were adorned with cracked posters declaring, in large black letters, "Interest on all goods sixpence" and "Please return ALL brown paper", the latter used to wrap large goods when they were, eventually, redeemed. One tiny window, set high in the wall, allowed a thin filter of daylight to creep in, serving only to emphasise the grimness of the room and dust mites dancing happily in the stale air. On leaving the building, looking to right and left before I turned onto the Coventry Road just in case any of my school-friends were about, I inhaled beautiful, clean breaths of pure, fresh air, slightly seasoned though it was by the smells from the pub!

Everyone we knew used the pawn shop, referred to as "Uncle's" if strangers were around when our parents were sending us there, such was the way of life then, but knowing that still couldn't stop me from feeling less of a person after being there. Father O'Keefe said that the "good Lord provideth for His children", and I often wondered if He knew about the pawn shop!

Gittens, the second-hand shop, filled me with horror! It was much used by most of the people in the area, especially at the start of a new school term! Some of the more affluent families used the "tally man; this was a man who came round from one of the big stores offering clothing on credit, but our family couldn't afford to pay him the required half a crown (twelve and half new pence) per week, so Gittens was our "shop". Its dull, brown painted window frames held glistening glass, obviously not at all ashamed of the shoddy goods

34

crouching on the other side. A discreet bell tinkled each time the door was opened, beckoning Mrs G to the smelly interior of her world.

In one corner of the wood-panelled room odd boots and shoes were piled haphazardly, their lace-less eyelets staring vacantly at the encroaching slim, white hands of Mrs G as she vainly searched for a matching pair. Sad fur coats hung drunkenly from a rusty rail, their proud exciting pasts buried forever beneath the now matted fur. "Gentlemen's Suits" held pride of place, each one hung on an individual wire coat hanger along the rear wall, their frayed cuffs and gaping buttonholes begging for the neatness of a tailor.

Overall hovered the smell! Mothballs, old cracked leather, sweat, despair, and now and then a hint of "4711 — Eau de Cologne", the latter waiting around the trim, blonde figure of Mrs G, seeming to seep into the articles cluttered around her.

Mrs G was a very friendly lady, totally at odds with her surroundings. I envisaged her serving on one of the beauty counters in a city centre store, so fitting for the dainty elegance she wore so effortlessly. One day, on my way home from school surrounded by other girls in my year, she called to me from her position on the cardinal polished doorstep of the shop. Colouring with embarrassment I shuffled over, head down, hands clenched tightly in the pockets of my green school mac (purchased from her shop the previous winter), and prayed harder than I ever had before: "Please, God, don't let it be something for me" when I beheld the brown paper wrapped parcel in her hands. Her words made me want

35

to curl up and die, especially when the other girls started giggling. "Tell your Mum just a shilling, dear" she smiled, and almost snatching the parcel from her I ran home.

My prayers weren't answered! On reaching home I watched with terror as Mother opened the parcel. Resplendent in their shoddiness lay a pair of dark brown leather, lace-up brogues! "Please, God," I prayed fervently, "I'll listen to everything Father O'Keefe has to say next Sunday, and I'll put some money in the plate instead of spending it on ice lollies, if You'll only not let them fit me!".

Once more I was disappointed. No matter how hard I tried to pretend they didn't fit, Father didn't agree. Fingering the beautiful leather in his work-worn fingers, almost reverently, he said "Sure, these will be fine when I've mended them, Mary. Now, hand me that last!". Trying to keep my tears at bay I did as he asked, and despite my abhorrence to the shoes, marvelled at the way his clever hands worked a miracle.

Shaping a piece of leather he found in his "cubby-hole", for he was a great believer in hoarding things that "might just come in useful some day", he proceeded to repair the shoes. Theresa and Chris cast me sly grins as he worked his magic, knowing full well they wouldn't fit either of them! When I got up the next morning there they lay, by the brass fender, soles pristine, uppers highly polished, the naked eyelets winking at me in the light of the fire. As I was about to comment that I couldn't possibly wear them without laces, Mother, a look of sympathy on her face, handed me a pair Father

36

had purchased from Maud's before he went to work that morning!

I swear those brogues were indestructible for, no matter how many kerbs I kicked, or how often I took them off and bashed them against a convenient wall, they survived. Each night Father sat in his chair in the corner, head bent at an uncomfortable angle, as he repaired whatever damage I had inflicted on them, just casting me a sorrowful look over his spectacles every now and then, making me feel very small indeed. Father O'Keefe chastised me severely when, finally, I confessed, weeks after I'd out-grown them and they'd been handed on to Theresa! She told me later she'd been praying for months that her feet would grow and grow so she would never have to wear the brogues. God didn't answer her prayers either!

To our amazement they lasted for about four years — due mainly I think to the loving care my Father lavished on them. He took great pride in our shoes, always ensuring they were highly polished and in good condition. He polished the uppers by melting a small piece of Cherry Blossom boot polish over the fire, once melted he patiently stroked it into the leather with a matchstick until it disappeared, which took absolutely ages. After leaving them down by the fender to dry out, he'd take a stiff, black brush, and briskly brush up the surface. Finally he used an old piece of soft cloth to bring them up to a better-than-new shine. After polishing the leather in between the sole and heel he declared them "fit for a King!", and he was right. No-one in our lane had more highly polished shoes than my family, due to the hours Father spent on his self-inflicted task. Father always said one could tell the "cut" of a person by the state of his shoes, and even to this day I ensure mine are always clean and shining!

Jumble sales were a constant source of delight to us, and we all loved browsing round, pushing through the crowds to get at the best "bargains". I loved buying the smelly, mildew-covered books, usually for around one old penny each, not caring that as I hugged them to my chest on the way home my clothes were getting badly stained. Granny Smith asked me once to try and get a nice "bit of something pretty" for her to drape over the back of the settee, in order to keep it free from the hair oil Young Tom wore. After searching for ages I emerged triumphantly from a scrummage at the "Material Stall" with a beautiful piece of tapestry, woven in shades of blue and gold and in almost perfect condition. Granny was thrilled, even though we found out later it was actually a cushion cover!

For some strange reason, or so I thought, our Jim always bought electrical goods, Heaven knows why being as we hadn't electricity! All was revealed years later when he told me he sold on the goods he purchased, making a profit in the process! Once he purchased a "new" wind-up gramophone, complete with a collection of Mario Lanza records, which gave us many years of pleasure. He loved buying things that he could take apart, to see how they worked, then, not always successfully, put them back together. He once tried his skills on Mother's prized possession, a beautiful, walnut-cased mantel clock, brought from her home.

Carefully he put all the cogs and screws on a piece of paper in the order in which he removed them. I don't know what went wrong, but after he'd put it back together again he had four small cogs left over! His explanation was that there had been far too many in the first place! Whatever the reason, that clock never worked again. Mother still has it but time has stood still in her living room, the hands set solidly at ten past two!

My love of jumble sales has never diminished, although now I browse happily amongst the books and games, delighting my grandchildren with my finds. The odd thing is that, no matter where the sale is held, the smell is exactly the same as when I was a child.

Our clothes, cast offs, second-hand, hand-me-downs, or whatever, may have seen far better days but they were clean. The smell of Reckitts Blue, which Mother put in the final rinse, gave our clothes a fresh, clean almost-new smell, which I adored, but it is the wonderful smell of shoe polish I remember best. Today when I polish the family shoes I recall the wonderful, pungent aroma of the Cherry Blossom polish my Father used, and although he has been dead for seventeen years the aroma brings him, and the dreaded brogues, vividly to mind.

CHAPTER
FIVE

Halls of Learning

Like a magpie I greedily stole
all the knowledge my brain could store,
never content with just a glimpse,
my soul cried out for More!

Avidly devouring all that I could,
even the mighty War and Peace!
Mother was worried that, some day,
my tired brain would cease.

Learning to me was pleasure untold,
filling my days with delight,
showing me a wonderful land
where everything would be right!

Education is food for the soul
assuaging the hunger to learn,
giving us hope to follow our dreams —
whichever way Life's path may turn.

Schools

Due to my feeble beginning I didn't actually start school until a few months after my fifth birthday, and was treated very much as the baby of the class. Not that I minded, it was lovely to be cuddled by our class teacher, who I always called Miss, and even now I can't remember her name!

Little Green Lane Infants and Juniors was quite a big school, built of red brick and reminded me of our church in a strange way, apart from the smell. Instead of the wonderful smell of incense the whole building reeked of cabbage! As I adored cabbage I didn't object to the smell. I also loved the smell of the lavender polish which the cleaners used to buff up the beautiful wooden floor of the school hall. I arrived early at school as my big brothers always dropped me off before going into their building. Alone I would stand in the vast emptiness of the hall, inhaling its delicious scents. A wonderful sense of joy filled my body as I relaxed in the peace and quiet, soon broken by hurtling bodies and shouts of the other children. At home there were so many of us that it was rare indeed to find any quiet moments.

My first few days were very confusing, but I loved everything about that school. Lessons were never a worry for me for I was eager to learn and would listen, captivated to the wonderful soft voice of my teacher. She was about forty then I suppose, small, rounded, with a kind face and twinkling blue eyes. If ever any of us were upset, as a lot of us were during the early days because we missed our Mothers, she cuddled us to her ample bosom, never chastising, always understanding. She always smelled of baby powder, I never understood why for I was sure she was far too old to have a baby at home.

My couple of years at the infant school were filled with fun, playing in the wendy house, singing, dancing as well as learning. I once played the part of Peter in the Golden Goose — which I really enjoyed until the afternoon I dropped the "egg". It was just as well that it was made of papier mâché as it fell on top of some of the other children. Miss soon dried my tears and, the following year, gave me a part in a play about a little gypsy girl named Gay. I yearned to play the main part, especially as I had black gypsy hair and the girl who played Gay had golden hair. I didn't really understand then that she was supposed to have blonde hair as she wasn't really a gypsy at all!

The junior school was, obviously, much bigger than the infants, with quite a few flights of stone stairs up to the classrooms, which resounded with the noise of hundreds of pairs of leather-clad feet! It smelled of chalk, ink and cabbage! How I loved writing with pens and pencils on pristine paper instead of with a piece of scratchy chalk on a slate as I had done in the infants. I loved the crisp, new smell of my exercise book and started each new page with the intention of keeping my handwriting neat all the way through — by the end of the first week my usual scribble had taken over.

I was quite overawed by the huge numbers of children milling around me, in the hall, the classrooms and the playground. Quite often I hid myself away in one of the toilets so I could have some peace from the noise and bustle. The toilets always smelled of bleach and red carbolic soap, the latter making my hands red and sore. The white roller towels were rough to the touch and smelled exactly the same as the toilets!

Unfortunately I was ill quite often during my early school years so missed out on a lot of the pleasures of school life. I wasn't allowed to do P.E., or take dancing lessons as the effort was just a little bit too strenuous for me. Some of the children mocked me, hinting that I was telling lies when I gave the teacher yet another exemption note from my Mother. If only they knew just how often I longed to be as fit as they were and enjoy all the things they took for granted.

The one thing I could indulge in was the annual fancy dress contest, how I loved it! One year my Mother made me a Little Red Riding Hood outfit, from scraps of material she had in a box and lots of safety pins. Sewing never was her strong point. Had it not been for one of the girls dressing up as Little Bo Peep, complete with "lamb" (her white cat), I am sure I would have won a prize that year! In my final year at the juniors I wanted to be someone completely different so one of Mother's friends, Edie, kindly loaned me a beautiful pure silk kimono that her late husband had brought back from his travels during his army days.

Mother and Edie spent hours piling my hair up into the typical "Geisha Girl" style, using long wooden knitting pins to skewer it in place. Tiny silver slippers, encrusted with beautiful embroidery adorned my feet, and I felt like a queen as I strutted in front of the mottled mirror of the chiffonier. With painstaking care Mother painted my face, following instructions from Edie, and then they both stood back to admire their handiwork.

Hobbling up the lane to the school, the kimono having been tightly bound with a huge, pale pink padded sash, I drew stares from everyone, and some ribald comments from the boys. At the tender age of eleven I did not understand half the comments then, but blush now when I remember them. None of the other girls stood a chance that day, and I tried not to feel proud when the headmaster called me on to the stage to receive first prize. I did thank my God the following Saturday when I went to Confession, and also admitted that I had, indeed, felt just the teeniest bit proud that day.

All too soon, or so it seemed, my junior days were over and I was on my way to the senior school — Tilton Road Secondary Modern Girls, and I loved it all from the very first day. Here I would learn it all, not just the three R's, but drama, dance, music, science, cooking, art, and I couldn't wait. My younger sisters thought I was mental to actually enjoy going to school.

Mrs Watts was the English and Drama teacher and I adored her. She was quite elderly even then, with snow-white hair highlighted with a blue rinse. Her tiny, bird-like features were lined, her mouth small but nearly always with a hint of a shy smile at the corners. She used a lace-edged handkerchief, sprinkled with Hartnell's "In Love", which we girls thought a strange choice for an elderly widow. I believed it was the perfume her late husband gave her and that was why she wore it.

When she spoke of Shakespeare her eyes would light up, her voice throbbing with the passion, and understanding, of the beautiful words. Through her eyes I saw the Bard working by candle-light, his feather quill gripped tightly in his artistic hands, words forming in his clever brain as quickly as they fell onto the parchment. Her lessons were the highlight of my school week, and I never, throughout my five years, did anything to receive one of her "black" marks, given out for various misdemeanours, but strived instead for "merit" marks, so much harder to achieve but worth it.

She seemed to have a soft spot for me and often spent many minutes, after class, talking to me about the work, my family life and her great love of Shakespeare. With her help I came to love his works as much as she did, but never quite grasped his meaning as quickly as she. She was interested in all her pupils, spending time with each of us, sometimes singly, sometimes in groups and, on occasion, inviting us to her home on Sundays to watch slides of the various theatrical productions she had produced at the school over the years. We were always invited to stay for afternoon tea, which consisted of small dainty cakes, thinly sliced buttered bread, various cheeses, weak tea in china cups, complete with saucers.

If the weather was fine we lay on the sweet-smelling grass in her beautiful garden, the scents of the various flowers and shrubs wafting over us, a haven of peace in our bustling world. My Father looked after the gardens during odd week-ends throughout the year, and admired Mrs Watts very much. She and my Father got on extremely well, and she often told me what a very intelligent man he was and, with a twinkle in her eye, would say it was a pity I hadn't inherited his brain!

She was interested in everyone and everything; when tragedy smote our family in the form of a still-born baby brother, she comforted me as a Mother would, rejoicing with us just twelve short months later with the birth of a beautiful baby sister.

Mrs Watts instilled in me a love of words, a gift which is always with me. She was the only teacher I knew who could command respect without raising her voice. All the girls adored her and looked forward to her classes and especially the drama group she ran every Tuesday evening.

I enjoyed many small parts in the plays she produced, and as I grew older was trusted with bigger and better roles, that of Jessica in *The Merchant of Venice*, although I secretly longed for the part of Portia so I could recite her "mercy" speech; Titania in *A Midsummer Night's Dream* and Viola in *Twelfth Night*. For the latter I was taken to a stage school in the centre of Birmingham to learn how to sword fence. On the opening night, a bundle of nerves, I forgot to put the protective cover over the point of my sword and to my everlasting shame actually stabbed the girl who played my opponent! Fortunately she wasn't badly injured but I treated the sword with far more respect during the rest of that week. It was a pity we were all girls there as I am sure the romantic parts, especially as we grew into adolescence, would have had more feeling if we had male actors! It was so difficult to portray love towards another female!

I loved the smell of the Leichner stage make-up but not the huge pots of goose grease Mrs Watts gave us to cleanse our faces after each performance. I believe it is because of all that grease I never came out in teenage acne!

At the age of fifteen I auditioned for a job with the Crescent Theatre in Birmingham and was lucky enough to be accepted. However it was not to be. My Father said I had to remain at school for an extra year to learn the intricacies of shorthand and typing, so my dreams of stardom faded into the walls of the typing room. In later life I did join an Amateur Dramatic Society, playing such parts as Lady Windermere, Fairy Happiness (in panto), a strange, elderly Irish maid in a thriller, plus numerous small walk-on parts, and so laid my earlier frustration to rest.

I hated science as much as I loved English, mainly because I was scared of everything in the Science Room! The science teacher, Mrs P, a fiery Italian lady, despaired of me ever learning anything. I was terrified of the dead frog she kept in her drawer, especially after she made one girl kiss it for misbehaving in class. The smell of the Bunsen burners, the strange coloured gasses, and the various chemicals always made me heave as they hit my nostrils. I couldn't dissect a frog, or a sheep's eyeball (ugh), make a "mini" explosion or even turn up with a complete flower for dissection. My friend, Pat, who lived in a nice house in Eversley Road, gave me a beautiful tulip from her garden for that particular lesson. Somehow, during our lunch-break, I managed to lose the head of the flower and entered the science room with just the stem. Mrs P was not amused and said I had no chance at all of passing my "O" level. I wasn't surprised, for I had no intention of taking it!

Mrs P had beautiful, reddish-brown curly hair, which frizzed out when she got annoyed. She wore beautiful clothes and always smelled of musk oil. Her long nails, were always painted with a pearly pink glossy polish, and as she demonstrated a test the pink tips glowed eerily in the light of the Bunsen burners. Her make-up was immaculate, and, judging by the delicious smell, it hadn't been purchased in Woolworth's. On odd occasions I have caught just a hint of that scent from a stranger and am immediately transported to the science room.

Cookery lessons were the bane of my life for, no matter how hard I tried, everything I attempted to cook was a disaster. Despite that I actually loved going into the huge, white cookery room, its ovens and work tops clinically clean, the wonderful smell of pies, stews and cakes lingering in the air. Even after the school holidays the room still smelled of whatever had last been cooked there!

Cookery was actually called "housewifery" in those days, I don't know why, unless it was because we were taught how to iron handkerchiefs etc. For the purposes of housework, and for the teachers to test our culinary skills, a small flat was available within the school grounds. I loved going in there, pretending it was my own home that I was making tidy for my husband coming in from a hard day's work. I was fascinated at how easy it was to use an electric iron for, at home, we had a flat iron which Mother put on the hob to heat, spitting on it to ensure it was hot enough to use! I loved the smell of ironing, so clean and fresh, but not the tangy smell when I burnt something, which was quite often, because I wasn't concentrating.

I day-dreamed the hours away in that little flat, trying to visualise what kind of home I would, eventually, share with the man of my dreams in the far, distant future.

My cooking left a lot to be desired, and still does unfortunately. Mine was usually held up as an example of how not to do things, but I didn't care. I was far more interested in reading, writing and acting. Mrs B, our "housewifery" teacher, would shake her head every time I walked into the cookery room, knowing that whatever I made would he a disaster, and she was never wrong. My poor Mother spent a fortune on the ingredients for beef goulash, chicken pie, fairy cakes, etc, but we were never able to eat anything that I produced. Unfortunately it was an essential part of the curriculum so I soldiered on for five years, and never once made anything edible.

Maths was my very worst subject and Mrs F would hand back my maths book every week with just a glint in her eye. I seemed to have a mental block when it came to figures, and couldn't understand why x equalled y or whatever, when as far as I knew shops dealt in pounds, shillings and pence then, which was easy for me to understand. At one point she banished me to the roof playground, not a hardship as it was a beautiful day and I could smell the wonderful aromas drifting across the roof-tops from Hughes Biscuit Factory! After she gave me the results of the mock "O" level, I achieved nothing out of one hundred per cent, she called me into her room and said "Tell your parents to save their money child, for you won't pass". In those days each RSA or GCE examination taken had to be paid for by the family, so I was glad I was saving my parents some of their hard-earned cash! My Father was disappointed, having spent many long, weary hours trying to make me understand what was, to me anyway, a foreign language! Denis too had tried to help me with my homework, finally giving up in exasperation!

My Father did all our sewing as Mother was quite inept with a needle, and I had obviously inherited her weakness. I managed to make a fairly recognisable sewing bag and a small sampler, and even mastered the art of smocking, after stabbing my fingers innumerable times. Miss S smiling at my pathetic efforts and doing her best to explain exactly what I was doing wrong, held them up to show the girls what I had achieved and then go on to point out the faults. This was never done in a malicious way, it was simply her way of ensuring the other girls didn't follow my example.

During our last school year we were allowed to make anything we chose, as long as it was "respectable". From my earnings as a Saturday girl at Woolworth's, I purchased a length of beautiful, silky-feel material in varying shades of blue, with cotton to match. and a pattern for a lovely, scoop-necked, tight-fitting dress, which I planned to wear at the School Leavers' Ceremony on our last day, blue being my favourite colour. After six weeks hard work I took the garment to Miss S for her approval. She was astounded and held it up for all the girls to see, praising me as she did so. I was so excited when she asked me to put it on so I could model it for the other girls.

Once in the cloakroom I struggled manfully, I knew it was meant to be tight, but not this tight I thought. I knew I hadn't put weight on, because I never did, and my five stone frame hadn't an inch of surplus flesh anywhere. Tears filled my eyes as I tugged and pulled and, eventually, managed to get the dress on. I hobbled back into the classroom, knees touching each other, feet turned in, stomach sucked in as far as it would go and, breathless, reached Miss S's desk. She rose to her full height of six feet and leaned towards me, her minty-scented breath floating under my nose, smooth brow puckered. Slowly she turned me this way and that, muttering under her breath.

A hush fell over the class as all the girls ceased their activities, eyes fixed on me and Miss S. "Oh dear, dear, dear" she exclaimed, "I thought it was too good to be true, you've left out a whole piece of this my dear!". Red-faced I shuffled back to the cloak-room, picked up my sewing bag and, sure enough, screwed up in a corner was what I had thought to be a spare piece of material. I didn't have the heart to finish that dress and the embarrassment has stayed with me ever since.

I must have learned something during those sewing lessons for, some years ago, I actually made six brides-maids' dresses, complete with underskirts and silky vest-tops, for my eldest daughter's wedding! I just wish Miss S had been there to see them.

My school days were very happy indeed and I couldn't stop crying on the day I left. Out into the big wide world we were being thrust, none of us feeling that we were ready, decisions to make alone, bosses to contend with, and it all overwhelmed me on that last day. Long after the rousing chords of "Jerusalem", the standard song for those leaving school, had faded into the ancient walls, I lingered, lost and forlorn. A gentle hand turned me round and the soft voice of Mrs Watts broke into my misery, "Don't cry, Mary dear" she whispered, her blue eyes suspiciously watery, "Don't think of this as the end of something, look on it as a beginning — the first day of the rest of your life". Her words did bring me comfort especially when she said "I shall miss you, dear, take care and do come and see me when you can". With a quick hug, and a dab at her eyes with the cologne-soaked handkerchief, she stepped away, shoulders hunched inside her smart grey linen dress. My eyes followed her retreating figure, stopping at the hall doors to turn and wave her handkerchief in my direction, causing a huge lump to form in my throat. Somehow I smiled, took a deep breath, pulled myself up to my full height of five feet two inches, smoothed down the beautiful lemon dress my parents had bought for this special day, and followed her out.

As I passed the cookery room I couldn't resist one last peep into the place which had been the scene of most of my scholastic disasters. A hint of flour, syrup and spice lingered in the quiet air and right in the middle of the huge wooden table sat an absolutely perfect cake, made by one of the second year's that day. Casting a quick look round, I walked up to it, tempted to break off a small piece of crust to taste. My God must have been sitting on my shoulder that day because I simply smiled and walked away, so allowing the unknown cook to receive the full marks she deserved. When I confessed my wicked thought to Father O'Keefe the next Saturday, he whispered, a smile in his voice, "Well done, Mary, but you know, no-body's perfect, not even me!", which made me feel a whole lot better!

I feel I was very lucky to have attended school then, and the pleasure, fun and excitement of learning stays with me. On visiting the schools of my children and grandchildren, and marvelling over their dexterity with computers, I hope they are finding the same camaraderie with their teachers that I found with mine, all those years ago.

CHAPTER
SIX

Remembering

Some faded photographs,
a rag rug on the floor,
big smile of welcome
as she opens the
door.

A jar full of pennies
right next to the sweets,
years filled with laughter,
and plenty of
treats.

Fine, white hair,
soft to the touch —
dear "Granny Smith"
we loved you so
much.

"Granny Smith"

Nearly all the children in the yard adopted Granny Smith, as their own grannies were either dead or lived too far away to visit very often. My granny (Mother's mother) lived in London where we spent our summer holidays so saw her for three weeks every year. Sometimes she visited us for just a few days, but as age and illness overtook her those visits ceased when I was quite young. My Father's Mother lived at home in Ireland so was just a face in a faded photograph.

Granny Smith was the epitome of what all grannies should be, being small and rounded, twinkling blue eyes in a smiling face, always treating us as if we were, indeed, her own grandchildren. We knew she didn't have any family, apart from "Young" Tom, the bachelor son who lived with her and who must have been at least sixty then.

She was a sweet lady of indeterminate years, with soft, wispy white hair, always dishevelled, almost as if she was continually caught in a storm. All the children loved her, partly because she gave us sweets, whispering "Don't tell the others", to whom she had already given their share!

I don't know where she came from for her voice held no trace of any accent! She didn't speak in a "posh" way, just unlike anyone else we knew. We were so used to the Brummie, Irish, Scots and Welsh accents in our area that listening to Granny's soft voice was a pleasant change, as we didn't have to strain to understand her!

On her way back from her twice-daily visits to the

toilet, she walked slowly back to her house, always stopping to pass the time of day with whoever was in the yard at the time. Her voluminous skirts and petticoats, tucked up inside the elastic of her long, pale blue or pink bloomers, brought many a titter from the children. With a withering look at the children, one of the adults kindly approached to say "It's snowing in the south again, Gran"! Blushing she hastily readjusted her clothing, shielded by the adult.

Whenever we ran errands for her, or brought her washing in, she always whispered "Pop in and see me later and I'll give you a little something from the jar". The jar, displayed for all to see on her highly-polished sideboard, contained lots of pennies, which she was always dipping into for the children. Our parents said we shouldn't take money from an old lady, but if we refused her face wrinkled up as if she was upset, so we very rarely heeded our parents instructions!

I loved going into her house, so different to ours. Because it was a front house it faced onto the lane, giving us an enticing glimpse of a world so different from the yard. From her front windows we watched the milkman feeding his horse with the sugar lumps Granny gave him, the post man, who always knocked on Granny's door to chat, and any delivery men making their rounds to the various shops. We also watched the children from the terraced houses across the lane playing on the bombed site, their shouts of joy reaching us through the open window.

The cream, lacy curtains which adorned her window, were soft to the touch and smelled of lavender all year round, the scent erupting from the small pots of that plant dotted along the sill. The pale grey, tiled, fireplace held an assortment of brass objects, a poker, a small shovel, a long thin rod with a stiff black brush on the end of it, and two dogs of a breed unknown to me. All these sat neatly on the hearth, gleaming in the fire's warm glow. The mantle-piece held an old-fashioned clock, its dark wooden case slightly scarred but polished to within an inch of its life. Small ceramic pots, filled with moth-balls, sat on either side of the clock, the cloying smell pervading the entire room.

The sideboard was covered in old photographs of ladies, dressed in long black skirts, their hair wound up into a variety of buns, and men in dark frock coats, high stiff collars stretching their necks to the limit. One of the ladies was Granny Smith's mother, but looked nothing like her, being tall and thin, with very sharp features. Another photograph was of her Father, who was exactly like Granny Smith. Their faces belied their personalities, Granny Smith once told me. Her Father was a typical Victorian male, very strict and ruled the family home with a firm hand. Her Mother, on the other hand, was soft and gentle, obviously her daughter had, fortunately, inherited her personality.

The centrepiece on the sideboard was a large glass vase, holding an array of flowers and ferns throughout the year, their delightful perfumes fighting for suprem-acy over the mothballs!

A dark brown, well-worn, leather three piece suite was grouped around the fireplace. One chair, much creased, was Young Tom's, and when he was out I loved to sit in it, for it was squashy and very comfortable. I dearly wanted to kick off my shoes, tuck my legs up underneath me and curl into it's soft comfort, but was much too shy to do so. Brightly coloured cushions, crocheted and knitted by Granny Smith, nestled along the backs of the settee and armchairs.

A small wooden table, covered with a dark red, chenille cloth jostled for space by the window, and was always set with cutlery and raffia place mats, almost as if the inhabitants were about to partake of a meal. A silver-plated condiment set reposed on a small, silver tray, each container always full, almost as if they were never used. Two dark brown, ladder-back chairs with faded tapestry seats, faced each other across the table. It was here Young Tom sometimes sat, oblivious to his surroundings, as he listened to the radio, which was usually kept on a shelf in the kitchen. He loved music and often, obviously forgetting we were there, turned up the volume as a particular favourite came over the air-waves. It was in that little room that I first heard classical music, so different to the "pop" hits I heard at Joan's house across the yard. Smiling, Granny Smith, cast fond looks at her son, tapping her fingers on the arms of her chair in time to the music.

In front of the fireplace was a faded rag rug, which Granny Smith told us her Mother had made many years before. When she spoke of her long-dead Mother her face softened into millions of tiny creases, her pale blue eyes almost disappearing as she thought of days gone by, a single tear the only evidence of her thoughts on the soft powdered cheek.

At such times Young Tom, his tall, thin slightly stooped figure clad in a maroon-coloured, sleeveless jumper, knitted lovingly by his Mother, pale grey shiny trousers, flopping at the knees, dark brown shoes encasing his long, thin feet, rose from his chair, dropped a kiss on Granny Smith's brow, then disappeared into the kitchen. Some minutes later he returned with a cup of hot, sweet tea, two Marie biscuits resting on the saucer, which he handed to his Mother, saying "Here you are, Mum, this will make you feel better". Tears clogged my throat whenever I witnessed his devotion, and I prayed that I too would he blessed one day with just such a son.

The furnishings were so different to our own, it was like being in another World. Despite the amount of furniture, it didn't seem cluttered for everything fitted, just like pieces of a jigsaw puzzle, and I always felt quite at home there. I loved the peace of that room, the ticking of the clock and Granny's gentle snores only adding to the atmosphere.

Granny Smith seemed quite content with her life, pottering around with the window boxes Young Tom had fixed on the kitchen windowsill, overflowing with colour all year round. He never returned empty-handed from his daily walks, showering his Mother with anemones, pansies, foxgloves, large daises, ferns and berries, which she immediately placed in the window-boxes. I loved standing by her back door just so I could absorb the wonderful aroma of fresh flowers!

Every winter Young Tom suffered with a weak chest, and the entire house smelled of Wintergreen ointment and sulphur! The remedies obviously worked for he was never indisposed for more than a week, as far as I remember. During his brief illness I went shopping for Granny, always amazed at the difference in their shopping list to our own. The fact that she always paid in cash also surprised me, for Mother said that pensioners were worse off than we were! I don't ever remember Granny or Young Tom going to the pawn shop or Raggy Allen's, so I believed they must have saved very hard for their old age.

From the Maypole on Coventry Road I purchased a small tin of pink salmon, half a pound of "best" (Golden Meadow) butter, one pound of sugar, a quarter pound of Typhoo tea, one packet of Marie biscuits and half a dozen "brown only" eggs! After taking this back to Granny, I then collected her weekly order of potatoes and vegetables from Wheelers, then to Maud's. Maud read the list, a box of sanitised toilet paper, one bar of Sunlight soap, a quarter pound of mint humbugs, one small "tin" loaf, (this was a square loaf — representing a bread tin in shape), one packet of Arrowroot biscuits, four ounces of "sharp" cheese and one ounce of Old Holborn tobacco "for Young Tom's pipe". When Maud read the last item she smiled, saying "I don't know why she has to put that on, for what else is Tom going to do with tobacco but smoke it!", shaking her turban-covered head as she advised me to go to the tobacconists for it.

Finally I visited Bywaters, the butcher's, holding my breath in an effort not to inhale the, to me anyway, obnoxious aromas of dead animals! I couldn't watch as the butcher weighed and wrapped up the liver, tripe, breast of lamb and shin of beef, heaving when he chopped off eight fat sausages from the dozens lying on the slab in front of me! Even worse than the smell of meat was the pungent aroma of wet fish, which Granny purchased from the "fish man" who called there every week. I couldn't stand the smell of it boiling away in her kitchen, masking the glorious aromas of the flowers and ferns.

I seemed to have a "knack" for hairdressing then, and was usually found on Saturday afternoons, once I'd finished any chores Mother decreed, either in Joan's bright, modern living room or Granny's cosy abode. Most Saturdays I washed and set Granny's fine, soft hair, gently rolling the thin strands around the metal dinky curlers, terrified lest I hurt her, Granny's scalp glowed pink through her hair, which I know worried her a great deal as before I did anything at all, she'd say "Try and cover mi bald patch, bab, don't want them old biddies down at the club talking about me!". Payment for my labours was in the form of a piece of high-smelling fish, which Mother promptly gave to Nigs, our cat, and something from the jar. On one occasion she gave me a pretty white cotton handkerchief, with tiny flowers embroidered all around the edges. I kept it in my box underneath the bed, and even after many years the smell of mothballs was still "ripe".

Joan was very fashion conscious, both in her dress and hair styles. I experimented on her hair, at her own request, with many colours and styles, always afraid I would ruin her "crowning glory". On one occasion I thought I had for it turned a deep shade of red, totally at odds with her pale auburn eyebrows and very white skin! To my amazement she was delighted, and gave me sixpence for my efforts! I enjoyed my self-inflicted tasks, mainly because, for just a short while, I could watch television in their cosy living rooms! I dreamed of one day becoming a hairdresser, thinking how wonderful it would be to create beauty with my clever fingers, winning awards and writing beauty columns in glossy magazines!

When Granny and Young Tom went off to their club, usually once a month, they were a sight to behold. Granny, dressed in a smart, floral, flowing dress in shades of blue or yellow, a mixture of her precious flowers fashioned into a corsage pinned on her chest, smart white pillbox hat, its veil floating level with her eyebrows, and awash with lavender water, was every inch the lady. She looked so beautiful, and in a lot of ways reminded me of the Queen Mother, although slightly older. Broadly she smiled, her false teeth gleaming from the good soaking they'd had overnight in bicarbonate of soda, waving at all and sundry as she waited at the top of the entry for Tom to appear.

Shyly that lovely man shuffled to his Mother's side, his lopsided smile wider than usual. With pride Granny looked up at her tall, not unhandsome, son. A dark brown pin-striped suit covered his sparse frame, the brilliant white of his shirt, topped by a starched pale blue collar, showing beneath the brown and white spotted tie tucked neatly into the waistband of his trousers, which he was continually hitching up. Dark brown, highly-polished shoes, their laces evenly tied, creaked as he walked, and the children tittered as Granny said, as she always did, "Oh, Young Tom, you'll have to stop polishing them, you know it doesn't do them any good!". Watching their progress up the uneven lane I smiled, returning Granny Smith's farewell wave, and inhaled deeply of the scents of lavender, fresh flowers and the hair oil Young Tom used to smooth down his unruly hair, which drifted into the air.

On washing days, Granny's line consisted of at least three pairs of pink bloomers, and the same of blue, Tom's "long-john's", white collar-less shirts, pristine white tea towels, which my Mother swore could never have been used, six starched collars and loads of large, square handkerchiefs, the latter obviously Young Tom's. I loved the smell of her washing, especially the nose-tickling tang of Robin's white powdered starch. When the weather was frosty Young Tom's long-john's, on being removed from the line, were stood against the outer kitchen wall until they'd thawed out! One night I got the fright of my life as I thought a ghost was standing outside Granny's window, breathing a sigh of relief when I realised that Granny had forgotten to take the long-john's in that evening!

Granny was very sad when I told her we were leaving the yard, as the Council were moving people out of the back-to-backs first. She cried softly, saying through her tears "I'll miss you, bab. Oh, why does everything have to change at my time of life!", and for the first time in all the years I'd known her I caught a glimpse of the fire and spirit she must have had when she was young — giving me a totally different view of the lady I knew so well.

Gripping my hand tightly in her soft, wrinkled one, blue eyes swimming with tears, she murmured "Thank you so much for keeping mi hair nice all these years", bringing a lump to my throat. With the well-known twinkle back in her lovely eyes, she laughed "I just wish that, wher-ever me and Young Tom end up, someone there will be able to hide mi bald patch!".

Sadly, we never saw either of them again, but I do pray that her wish came true.

CHAPTER
SEVEN

Penny Waste

I remember, oh so well,
the aromatic smell
of new-baked loaves,
fresh from the stoves
of the baker in our lane.

And, again, I can recall
queuing along the wall
for the "penny waste"
and, oh! the taste,
it lingers in me yet.

No, I never will forget
the baker down our lane.

Food, Glorious Food!

The smells from Wimbush bakery haunted us all throughout our childhood, and we loved them. We children would stroll past the metal, roll-over doors of the bakery simply so we could inhale the mouth watering aromas of new-baked bread, cakes etc. Once a week they sold off slightly "imperfect" bread and cakes, I think it cost one shilling (five new pence), although I always called it "Penny Waste".

Sometimes we'd be lucky and find a whole cake, or bun, in the bottom of the bag, which we'd share with whoever was with us at the time, before taking the remainder home. It seemed then, no matter how much we ate, we were always ready for more!

At both Easter and Christmas the bakery excelled in the delightful aromas which wafted over the grimy chimney-stacks, through the "snug" of The Cricketer's Arms public house, up through the very earth of the bombed sites to tease around the edges of the ill-fitting window frames of the old, worn back-to-back houses in which we lived, before settling in the corners of every room of the houses.

A piece of crusty bread, spread with dripping, or jam in more affluent times, and a bowl of thick, creamy porridge started our days in Winter. In Summer we still had the bread and dripping, and if Mother could afford it golden, crunchy cornflakes, smothered in sugar and milk. At lunch-time we usually had "hutney dutney", which was day-old bread soaked in hot water, left to stand for a short while, then all the moisture squeezed out, sugar and margarine added, and the piéce de resistance — hot milk! It was delicious, but my own children thought otherwise when I tried to tempt them one day, many years later.

In the evenings we usually had bone stew, and I can remember the embarrassment I felt on having to ask the butcher for a bone "for the dog" — we didn't have a dog, as he well knew! Mother would put the bone in a huge saucepan which hung over the fire, adding carrots, onions, swede, turnips, parsnips, cabbage, potatoes, salt, pepper and Oxo cubes. The mouth-watering aroma filled our stomachs long before they knew the joy of the flavour. Sometimes Mother would boil a bacon hock, which I abhorred. The pungent smell reminded me so forcibly of the scenes, and scents, of the slaughterhouse, where I'd watched the pigs being slaughtered.

Sometimes we had fried egg and mashed potatoes with fresh peas, eating far more peas as we shelled them than ever went on our plates. The delicious aroma of an egg fried in dripping cannot be beaten and the taste is beyond description. In those days we hadn't heard of cholesterol, and wouldn't have cared anyway if it meant missing out on some of the wonderful concoctions Mother created! My most favourite meal was "curly kale", this was dark green cabbage, cooked until soft, then mashed up with creamy potatoes, a knob of butter, a hint of pepper and salt, and eaten with a piece of bread and butter. We didn't have a lot of meat as it was very expensive, especially when it ceased to be rationed, but Mother had a great flair for producing "miracle" meals out of very little.

Occasionally Mother cooked tripe and onions, or pigs' trotters, the latter being a particular favourite of my Father. My stomach would heave at just the thought of eating the dirty-white, wobbly mess that was tripe, or the pointed feet of a pig! As I had a "delicate" tummy I was more fortunate than my siblings, for I never had to partake of such foods. Tucking into my delicious curly-kale I'd cast a sly grin at the rest of my family, suffering the dubious delights of tripe and onions! Each time I told Father O'Keefe, during Confession, how relieved I was not to have to eat such things, he would shake his shaggy head, whispering "Was it the tripe again, child?". Slowly he would make the sign of the cross, murmuring "Sure your brothers and sisters will rest easy in Heaven, but, you, my child, shall rest easy on Earth!". I never did understand what he meant by that, but just assumed he was on my side!

Hughes Biscuit Factory, behind Tilton Road School, emitted the haunting smells of spice, ginger and fresh baked dough, their scents drifting over the tip, across the "cut", through the age old walls of our school, and into the very tarmac of our playground. Every Saturday children from all around gathered outside there for a free bag of broken biscuits. The unwritten rule was one bag per family, yet all five of us joined the queue, the sixth family member being too young at the time, but no-one ever said anything. As everyone else did the same I suppose it wasn't really cheating, for surely the people who owned the factory would have done something about it. Most families then consisted of at least four children, one family in our lane had eleven, and with only the husbands working, usually on low wages, any food was more than welcome.

On Saturdays, after I'd finished my other "chores" I accompanied Mother up to the Coventry Road for the shopping she wouldn't purchase from Maud's. Looking back I suppose it was because she didn't want Maud to know of the "luxury" items she purchased from the shops on the main road. First to the Maypole, the general store, millions of smells similar to those in Maud's shop but magnified a hundred times, drifted into the air, where we purchased one packet of "best" butter (Mother's only weakness), a bit of unsmoked back bacon for Father and half a dozen "just laid" eggs. These were really big and brown, and even today I always look for brown eggs as I know the flavour is much richer. We purchased huge "bloomer" loaves from Wimbush, their rich freshness making my mouth water.

One day, I was about fourteen I suppose, Mother, laden down with shopping, suddenly stopped right outside Wimbush bakery where the men were taking a well-earned rest. Her face red, she muttered "Stand in front of me, child, for Heaven's sake!". Mystified I did as she asked, my face turning red when I realised the elastic had given way in her blue bloomers, which were now hanging from her knees to her ankles. Hastily she stepped out of them and shoved them inside one of the bags, next to the bread. Both blushing furiously we scurried up the lane, to the ribald comments and jibes of the now-laughing men! To this very day my Mother pins her knickers to her corset to ensure such a thing could never happen again!

At last we came to my most favourite shop ever — Stockton's Pie Shop in Greenway Street. Most of the people in the area called it simply The Apple Tart Shop. The rich, spicy, mouth-watering aroma of cooked apples reached us before we were even half way to the shop, and my taste buds would erupt with just the thought of the treat in store. The queues were always long, nearly half way down Greenway Street, but no-one seemed to mind at all, as knowing that in just a short while we would actually be eating one of the delicious tarts was a pleasure in itself. On entering the shop the aroma became more pronounced, mingling with the smells of the meat and potato pies also cooked there, and I found it very hard indeed to stop myself from drooling over the golden-crusted wares.

Most of the time we could only afford one "family sized" apple tart, which just about satisfied us all. It cost one old shilling (five new pence), plus a penny for the loan of the tin plate on which it sat. As long as we returned the plate the next week there would be no charge for a fresh plate.

On reaching home Mother would put the kettle on the gas, humming a happy little tune as she laid out the cups and plates on a tin tray, and we children would sit, as if mesmerised, by the sight of the wonderful tart taking pride of place on the scarred wooden table top. With a cup of tea, and a slice of the still-hot apple tart clutched in my hand, my cup of joy was full.

The forbidden fruits of the outdoor, on the corner of Little Green Lane and Arsenal Street, drew us like a magnet. I enjoyed the tangy aroma of the homemade ginger beer the elderly Licensee's wife made up, tall, frothy jugs lining the counter-top, but was never allowed to taste it.

When I finally did sample the bottled variety I was sadly disappointed — it tasted just like soap to me! The strong, minty scent of the shiny, black and white humbugs, within tempting reach in open topped jars, but out of our price range, lingers still in my memory. I also adored the musky, salty tang of the one penny bags of crisps, with the magic, blue bag of salt tucked right down at the bottom. The sweet, rich smell of Old Holborn tobacco filled the air as the Licensee sucked contentedly on his pipe, his rheumy eyes smiling at us through a haze of blue smoke.

Arrow toffee bars, for just one old penny, liquorice sticks, gob-smackers (huge round balls of some hard, sweet substance that lasted for hours), aniseed balls — when eating the latter none of the other children came near as the smell was so overpowering, and ever-lasting sticks of toffee. "Traffic-light" lollies, each stripe containing a different flavour, delicious tangy orange ice lollies, Walls vanilla ice-cream, the choice was endless on Friday nights at Whites newsagents where we chose to spend our long-awaited penny! Even now my taste-buds are reacting to the memories.

On bicycle rides with my Father, to Meridan, Coventry and wherever else the mood took us, we'd eat an abundance of the berries found on the hedges along the way, blackberries, strawberries and gooseberries, all growing wild and there for the taking. Replete, we lay against a convenient haystack recovering both from the ride over the then pot-holed Coventry Road and the surfeit of fruit. Sometimes we would purchase an ice-cream from the candy shop by the monument in Meridan, leaning against the stone and idling the hours away.

During these precious days with my Father he told me of his childhood home, bringing to life a land I had yet to see. Through his eyes I saw the tiny cottage, the beautiful mountains, the rippling streams, his parents, and I longed for the day when we would travel to his boyhood home together. As dusk descended we remounted our bikes and headed for home, saddlebags filled to bursting with fruit just waiting to be "magicked" into delicious pies by Mother.

The fish and chip shop, at the Arsenal Street end of Greenway Street, was another source of delight to us. Every Friday, as soon as Father put Mother's money on the table, she'd hand me a ten shilling note (fifty new pence) and send me there for the usual four pennyworth of chips and a piece of fish. The smell assailed me before I'd even left the yard, and I'm sure even a stranger, with his eyes shut, could have found his way to that fish shop. Once inside the moist, aromatic warmth of the shop I'd rue the fact that, of all my siblings, I was the only one to be allergic to fish! Huge pieces of cod, covered in golden batter, thick and crusty, and soaked in salt and vinegar nestled closely to the big, fat, succulent chips, cooked in dripping. With the newspaper wrapped bundle clutched tightly to my chest I raced home, grateful for the warmth seeping through the paper on cold, winter evenings.

Once home Mother shared out the chips, placing a huge piece of warm crusty bread alongside, then carefully divide up the fish. How she managed to feed eight of us with such a meagre amount I'll never know, but she did. I know the story of the loaves and fishes very well, and often thought Mother performed her own miracle every Friday night!

Nigs, the cat, sat on Father's shoulder, his paw flicking out each time Father attempted to put some fish in his own mouth. I think Nigs got more of it than Dad did!

As I write this I can see Mother bent over the table, the light of the gas mantle casting a reddish glow over her beautiful auburn hair, soft face set in lines of concentration as she ensured we all received the same amount, and her smile as she finally sat down which seemed to say "We've made it through another week!".

CHAPTER
EIGHT

Football Crazy!

In blue and white
scarf,
"rattle" in hand,
I sang
and cheered
with the rest
of the fans.
For years I have
waited
to be part
of the crowd,
noisy, excited,
shouting
out loud
as goals
are scored,
one,
two
and three —
by the
other team,
unfortunately!

St. Andrew's

A pall of gloom hung over the whole of Small Heath, in fact the whole of Birmingham and the footballing world. Jeff Hall, right-back for Birmingham City, and just twenty nine years old, had tragically died. He was one of the Blues' brightest stars, having been capped for England seventeen times in his short career.

I was upset that someone so young, and obviously very fit, could be stricken by Polio, believing it to be a disease of childhood and hadn't realised, until then, that everyone was vulnerable. At that point in my young life I hadn't encountered Death so couldn't identify the strange, lost feelings I suffered when I read in the Evening Despatch of the tragedy.

Mrs H, an avid Blues supporter, cried for days, a forlorn, keening sound which affected all of us. "He was a lovely young man!" she pointed out to everyone, "and such a brilliant player", breaking into more heart-rending sobs. Jeff's death affected my eldest brother, Denis, very badly, and although I hadn't at that point, actually been to a match, I felt his sorrow. He moped about the house for days after Jeff's funeral, his sad face a constant reminder of the tragedy, and I prayed hard to my God to give him back his sense of fun.

Although Jeff wasn't Birmingham born, the city had taken him to their hearts and my heart wept for his family. How proud they must have been of his achievements, and how distraught they must be at such an unexpected end to their son's life. That he died on a Saturday I found particularly moving, but I couldn't understand how the sun kept shining, it was a particularly mild day, when something so dreadful had happened to one of God's children. I was relieved there wasn't a match that day for I felt sure that all his teammates wouldn't have wanted to play without him there. It was a very sad, bleak time and I prayed for something nice to happen to lift the gloom.

A memorial, in the form of a score-board and a clock, were erected in Jeff's memory. The score-board, as far as I know, is still there today, but I don't know what happened to the clock. It doesn't seem much to remember such a great player, but then I'm just a female!

It was strange to think that the Blues team was formed by a group of cricketers, from Holy Trinity Cricket Club in Bordesley Green, looking for a winter pastime, way back in the 1800s. The team was known as Small Heath Alliance, and in 1905, during a dinner party at the Swan Hotel in Yardley, the name was changed to Birmingham City Football Club. For some reason people were not keen on the "City" part of the name so the team was known, for a long time, simply as Birmingham Football Club.

In Little Green Lane there is a pub called The Cricketer's Arms, and I often wondered, as a child, how it came to have such a name. It obviously had something to do with the Holy Trinity Cricket Team I suspect.

Mrs H was a great source of information when it came to her beloved Blues. Her husband and son weren't interested in football at all, which we thought was strange, as most families supported our local team. On match days, a blue and white striped hat perched jauntily atop her short black hair, scarf wound round her thin neck, looking quite incongruous over the long black coat, with the hem of her pleated black skirt showing many inches beneath, a fresh bunch of violets or freesias pinned to her coat lapel, she tripped down the yard, black, leather-soled shoes resounding on the cobbles. With rattle in hand she would say "I'm off to see our boys win — see you later!", and with a sweep of her skirt, a shake of her rattle she disappeared down the entry.

It seemed a very strange hobby for a lady of indeterminate years, very elegant, quietly spoken, and I never could visualise her shouting her lungs out with all the men! On her return from the match, flowers wilting, scarf billowing over her shoulder, brown eyes alight, she would say, quietly, "We won!", then disappear indoors to prepare her husband's tea.

She spoke knowledgeably about the players, as if she was a personal friend to them all! I know she attended many of their social functions for, some time before, I'd puzzled for days when she told Mother that she'd "been on the floor all night". Later I learned she'd been dancing with the Blues players. She spoke with awe of Merrick, Houghton, Scholfield, and of the team's glorious win against Sunderland (6-1) in 1958, and of her disappointment when they lost to Manchester City in the F.A. Cup in 1956. Bert Trautmann broke his neck during that match but still carried on playing!

My earliest memories of football was the rush to "save" cars on a Saturday when the Blues played at home. For just sixpence we offered to "mind" innumerable cars, sneaking off home as soon as the supporters were out of sight! Nearly every car in those days was black, and even the oldest was clean and cared for. I loved to run my hands along the sleek, shiny bonnets, the faint smell of polish lingering on my fingers until tea-time. Most of the men would smile, funny how all the drivers were men then, never seeming to mind my grubby fingers, and hand over a shiny sixpence. Sometimes we weren't paid until after the match was over, something we weren't too keen on as, if Blues lost, none of the men were inclined to pay up! If anyone dared not to pay us, they suffered for it the next week as we'd pretend all the spaces were booked and paid for by someone else! When I confessed that particular sin to Father O'Keefe he didn't have a lot to say, just gave me a short penance and whispered gruffly "You'll learn, child, you'll learn!".

From our yard we could hear the cheers when goals were scored, and the very air in Small Heath would be filled with excitement so tangible one could almost feel it — I could certainly smell it! Some of the boys would race along to the homes of friends in Garrison Lane, there to climb on the roofs of the toilets in the hope of seeing into the ground. I often wished I was a boy so I could join them! Our Jim climbed to the top-most point of the tip in order to catch a glimpse of what was going on.

During my fifth year at school I sometimes accompanied some of the girls, during the lunch-break, to the Garrison Lane entrance of St. Andrews, in the hope of seeing our heroes. The gate-keeper often pretended he didn't see us, turning his back so we could "sneak" past him. I saw Bertie Auld and Jimmy Bloomfield, albeit from a distance, and hugged the knowledge to myself in case our Jim told Mother!

The younger girls were green with envy when we regaled them with tales of the discussions we had with the players! All told for effect of course, in my case anyway, for I would simply have fainted away if one of them had really spoken to me!

I loved the blue and white hats and scarves the supporters wore, and longed for the day when I could show I was a true fan. I tried for years to get Denis to take me, but to no avail. He was far too grown-up to be seen with his little sister at a match. I despaired of ever seeing my heroes so contented myself with reading all the match reports in the local paper, excitement churning in my stomach if we won, searing disappointment filling my soul if we lost. Sometimes Mrs H would let us watch the sports news on her television, especially when Blues were on, so I lived, second-hand, the joys and excitement of a football match.

Mother couldn't understand why I was so interested in football, considering I couldn't participate in school sports. Patiently I explained I didn't want to play the game simply be able to go and watch, cheering and shouting with everyone else. I thought it was marvellous that we had our own football team, just around the corner, and felt that everyone should support them!

My chance came, at last, in 1963. Some Friday nights my parents took me out with them to a favourite pub of theirs in the city centre, The Birmingham Arms. I quite fancied Gwyn, the middle son of the Licensee, and tried all my girlish "wiles" to lure him, but was beginning to despair of ever going out with him.

One evening, we were helping his father to clean up, I stepped outside the double glass doors of the bar to lock the outer, wooden ones, but couldn't reach the bolt. The boy of my dreams came out to assist, and suddenly the glass doors were bolted behind him. His father, knowing we were both too shy to show we cared, had locked us out on purpose, for he called through the closed doors "Now you can ask her out, son!".

Embarrassed I looked down at my feet, casting surreptitious glances at Gwyn, puzzled when I saw him gazing at the stars. Quietly he muttered, "It should be a good day for the match tomorrow!". Heart leaping in my breast I said, quite casually I thought, "Are you a Blues supporter too?", knowing full well he was, having gleaned every bit of information from his sister! The upshot of it was he asked me to go with him the next day to see Blues play Sheffield Wednesday, and my excitement knew no bounds.

It rained heavily the next day, and no matter how much I protested that I didn't mind standing in the rain to watch the match, Gwyn said he wouldn't expect it of me. Disappointed we went to The Futurist cinema, my clothes soaking wet, the fake fur collar of my coat emitting a strange, musty smell — I think it came from my being over-zealous with Mother's Rosewater cologne before leaving the house! Although I was happy to be, at last, going out with Gwyn, I was sorely disappointed that, once again, my dream of seeing the

Blues in the flesh was denied me. On leaving the cinema we learned the match had resulted in a draw, so I wasn't as disappointed as I would have been if we'd won!

During the days of our courtship many things transpired to prevent my going to a match, and I finally relinquished my child-hood dream, which was resurrected on December 28th 1963. My birthday is on Boxing Day, and as a treat Gwyn took me to watch to our team play Arsenal. My excitement knew no bounds as I put on my blue and white scarf and "bobble" hat (purchased during my days as a Saturday girl, but never yet worn), preening in front of my bedroom mirror. My sisters all thought I was mad to actually want to stand out in the freezing cold, the day after Christmas. I didn't care — all I could think of was that I was actually going to fulfil a long-held dream that day.

It was freezing, but the heat of the bodies in the queue, all the men much taller than me, helped a little bit. Once inside the ground I wanted to shout out my joy for all to hear! The smell of hot-dogs, damp clothes, and clean, cold air assailed me and I loved every bit of it. The men on the terraces kindly moved me along to the end of the row so I could watch the action. I actually ended up standing on the steps dividing the terraces, to avoid getting a crick in my neck.

My whole being was filled with so much joy and pleasure I thought I would burst! I was very surprised at the size of the ground, and the number of people who had turned out on such a cold day. Gwyn told me the usual "gate" for a Blues match was between 35,000 to 40,000, even more when cup matches were played. I don't know how many were there that particular day, only that as one man swayed so did everyone else, causing a wave-like roll along the terraces. Seeing me clasp my arms to my body to try and keep warm, an elderly man at the end of one row handed me a bright blue flask, saying "Take a drink of that, love, it'll warm you up"! After taking off the cap, and unscrewing the plastic cup, the delicious beefy aroma of oxtail soup drifted into the still, cold air. Greedily I gulped down a whole boiling mouthful, before remembering that I hated oxtail soup! Well, until that moment, I thought I did!

It was a wonderful experience, and I was totally surprised when, suddenly it seemed, it was all over. I had shouted, stamped, cheered, booed, sang, whistled, and jumped up and down each time a goal was scored, becoming so excited I even cheered when Arsenal scored! I didn't cheer for them again — they beat us 4-1!

The best, most memorable part of that day for me was when, towards the end of the match, everyone started to sing "Keep right on to the end of the road", thousands of voices singing as one and tears filled my eyes. As we left the ground, Gwyn's arm around my shoulder, one man patted me on the head as he passed and said, "Don't cry, bab, we don't lose 'em all!". Smiling through my tears I didn't bother to explain why I was crying, as I don't think he would have understood!

Walking back to the Birmingham Arms, the cold winter air seeping into my bones, the smells from the discarded hot-dog wrappers drifting into my nostrils, I couldn't stop talking about the match. At last I understood why men loved football so much — not only for the excitement it created in what was, for most people then, a very hard life, but for ninety short minutes they could let off steam, pretend they were out there on the pitch, scoring goals, the peoples' heroes!

Whole families attended at Blues matches in those days, children as young as eight or nine accompanied by at least two, sometimes three, of the older generation, knowing they were quite safe. There was never any trouble as far as I remember, no matter how big the gate. We were so lucky having a great football club just around the corner.

On our wedding day, August 29th 1964, Gwyn's first words to me as I reached the altar were, I suppose, not really surprising,: "They've just kicked off!". As we exchanged vows amidst the scent of lily of the valley, roses and incense, I smiled, so glad I was marrying my soul-mate! Blues may have lost that match, to Stoke City, but our "match" is still going strong, and in a roundabout way it's all thanks to the Blues! Long may they reign!

CHAPTER
NINE

Confession

With trembling knees and thumping heart,
and nails chewed to the quick,
I'd fiddle with my Rosary beads,
feeling very sick!

When my turn came to confess,
my voice would disappear,
until the Father whispered
"Why don't you speak up, dear."

So ashamed, and contrite,
I'd confess my wicked deeds,
all the while my fingers clutched
the smooth and hallowed beads.

At last, renewed, I'd say my prayers,
as all good Catholics should,
promising Him I would try
always to be good.

I know I didn't take it seriously,
this baring of the soul,
so, why, when I had confessed
did I go home feeling Whole?

Piety

The Holy Family Church, on Coventry Road where Small Heath joined Hay Mills, was a beautiful building. Its stained glass windows always seemed to glow with an inner fire. The smell of incense invaded every corner, even the Confessionals, and I would inhale its essence, feeling pure and holy. The flickering candles in their beautiful, wrought-iron stands, wax dripping like tears down their stems, cast wonderful shadows on the walls, highlighting the perfect faces of the glorious statues. St Theresa, the Little Flower, her marble feet draped with flowers, was my favourite Saint at that time. Her face seemed more serene than the Virgin Mary, her eyes kinder and softer somehow. Each time I passed her I touched her feet, which were surprisingly warm, and a little shiver would run up and down my spine, as if to say she knew exactly who I was.

Although my parents never attended Church, except for christenings, weddings and funerals, they ensured we attended every week as soon as we were old enough to be entrusted to the care of our elder siblings. I loved the entire scenario of our faith, from those beautiful glittering, candles, the windows, the haunting smell of incense and even the moth-ball scented cassocks of our Priests.

The one thing I wasn't too keen on was taking lots of other children with me to Sunday Mass, even the youngest baby in her pram. During the service she needed feeding and changing and Father O'Keefe would stare down at me from the pulpit, eyes glittering. He never said anything, I suppose because he knew my Mother needed a rest on a Sunday morning!

Sometimes we were late arriving so couldn't actually get into the Church so would have to go into the school hall instead. The latter was used for services at weekends as the Church itself would be filled to over-flowing. I didn't like the school hall, mainly because the scents were so mundane, just like our own school hall. I never felt uplifted or holy when I had to attend a service in there.

On the Saturday before Christmas, after having made Confession, I would walk on tip-toe, afraid to break the hushed silence, to where the nativity scene was set out to one side of the altar. Peace washed over me as I gazed at the baby doll lying in the wicker crib, the bright silver star, lit from behind, casting its eerie light over the figures reposing by Him.

We attended Confession every month, I don't know why because I can't really remember committing any "heinous" sins! One Saturday, on the way home from Confession, our Jim was teasing me, as he usually did, and I lost my temper and called him a cow! As soon as we got home he told Mother who, after blessing herself innumerable times and calling on all the Saints to "preserve us", and sprinkling holy water on my head, she sent me all the way back to Church to "cleanse my soul" again!

Father O'Keefe had taken the confessions that day and was just on the verge of leaving the Church when I raced in, breathless. "What did you want, child, did you forget something?" he asked, his deep voice rumbling in his chest. I stared up at his tall, square figure, shaggy, grey hair adorning his head, a frown between his bushy eyebrows. Nodding, for I was too out of breath to speak, he took me by the elbow and escorted me into the Church. "Was it your prayer book, Mary?" he asked as he ushered me down the aisle. Trembling I whispered "No, Father. My Mother sent me back, for I've to confess something to you", shrinking as he turned, eyes suddenly steely blue.

Without saying another word he disappeared into one of the Confessionals, beckoning me to follow. On legs that suddenly seemed to have developed the "St. Vitus' Dance" I crept into the Confessional. Even the smell of incense didn't soothe my troubled soul that day as he said, sternly, "Didn't I absolve you just an hour ago?". My voice trembled as I whispered "Yes, Father, but Mother said I must tell you that I swore on the way home!". Through the mesh of the confessional I could see his large face looming closer and I shrank back. "Swearing now is it, well, come on then, out with it. What did you say?". Blessing myself I repeated exactly what I'd said to our Jim, and why.

"Cow, did you say child?", he asked now, his voice sounding strangled. With tears running down my face and head sunk on my chest I confirmed my sin. In the sudden silence that followed my confirmation, I looked up to see his huge shoulders shaking behind the not-quite-concealing mesh. "Well now", recovering himself, "just go and say one Hail Mary and promise me you won't call your Jim a cow again?".

Grateful to have been let off so lightly I made to leave

the tiny room. He whispered, "Next time you're annoyed with him, don't call him a cow, call him a bull — for I think you must have offended his male ego!", and with a spluttering cough he blessed me and sent me on my way.

Everything looked so beautiful the day I made my First Holy Communion, the church was awash with flowers, their delightful scents mingling beautifully with the age-old incense. As I walked down the aisle the mixed aromas made me feel light-headed and I felt as though I was in a dream. I don't remember much about the actual ceremony, except that my younger sisters looked on with envy. At the grand old age of seven I suddenly felt older and wiser than all of them! So caught up was I in the beautiful service, the colours, the smells and the wonderful singing of the Nuns, that I told Father O'Keefe that I too, would be a Nun one day. He simply smiled, patted me on the head and went to talk to some of the parents.

As I grew older I craved the inner peace I always felt in my church and yearned for the serenity of the Nuns. Their gentle ways and their closeness to God intrigued me and I longed to know the secrets they surely knew. I don't know when I began to have doubts about joining a religious order but think it may have been when I saw the film *The Nun's Story*, starring Audrey Hepburn. I was aghast at how hard her life seemed and cried copious tears when she was punished by the Mother Superior. Fortunately I hadn't promised God I would become a Nun, only Father O'Keefe and he seemed to have forgotten all about it, for which I was truly thankful.

In order to be prepared for my Confirmation I attended weekly sessions with Father O'Keefe at the presbytery. I found it so difficult to remember my Catechism, so distracted was I by the bustling little body of Mrs Beesley, the housekeeper, as she fluttered backwards and forwards through the huge, oak-panelled hall carrying steaming dishes for the Fathers' lunch. The aroma of roast beef and Yorkshire pudding, boiled hams and Irish stew would seep into the small, book-lined room where I received my instructions, causing my stomach to rumble and my mouth to water. Many times I tried to extend the lesson by being deliberately slow in understanding just in case Father O'Keefe should invite me to join him for lunch, but he never did.

As we had to have a Saint's name for our confirmation name I spent hours testing the various names I loved, toying with such names as Sylvia, Wendy, Susan, all names I had seen in books. Unfortunately there didn't appear to be any Saints by those names. My Mother wanted me to have Philomena, a name I abhorred. In tears I approached Father O'Keefe who, fortunately agreed wholeheartedly with me! Eventually we decided on Monica, the mother of Saint Augustine, and one which I thought would fit nicely with my Christian names of Mary Margaret. I regretted it throughout the rest of my school days for I was ever after known as either Mildly Mad Mary or Moni-Mary! I can't mention some of the other unsavoury nick-names!

When I was very young, about seven or so, I attended

Sunday School, which was held in the hall of Little Green Lane Infants. I loved going for we used to sing all the lovely hymns and I was always chosen to sing solo, something I loved. One Sunday the teacher said I could sing a song of my own choice and I was thrilled. Mother used to sing all the time so I knew loads of songs even then. I thought the one I chose was quite good, it started off "I'm very like my Father in everything I do, for he's a little common-sense and I've a little to. Oh I mean to take things easy this World to travel through for my Father used to do it and I'll do it too". The teacher was smiling, and tapping her feet in time to the rhythm until I got to the bit "I like a smoke of tobaccy, I like a pint of beer". In horror she threw up her hands, exclaiming, "Oh, no, Mary, I don't think that's a nice song at all!". When I told my Mother she smiled wryly, saying "Oh, I do wish you had told me what song you were thinking of", on seeing my woebegone expression she hugged me and said "Oh, don't fret, child, we'll teach you a nice one for next Sunday", and she and my sisters grinned at each other across the table.

Our Jim heard of a Sunday School class which was held in a Methodist hall every Sunday evening, having sneaked in there one night. He regaled me with tales of how wonderful it was, how nice the preacher was and the lovely games they played, and best of all the food they had after each session. He hadn't told our parents that it wasn't a Catholic class, simply that it was "religious" so they allowed me to accompany him.

On my first visit I was a bit disappointed at how shabby the exterior was, so unlike our own magnificent church. The interior was not much better, being a large cold room, bare of anything except chairs, and reeking of some kind of disinfectant. Where were the flowers and the exotic scents, the wonderful flickering candles whose fatty smell drifted into nostrils and into our very soul? This indeed was a very strange religion I thought then, without any beauty or joy.

The preacher was quite young, I suppose about thirty or so, although to me he seemed very old. He wore wire-rimmed spectacles perched on the bridge of his nose, which was long and straight. I never saw him without a smile on his face, or lose his temper with any of us. He was obviously pleased that so many children flocked to his class, unaware that part of the attraction was the food. Small plates of boiled egg sandwiches, one of my favourite foods, tiny currant cakes, crumbly biscuits and small paper cups of watery orange pop reposed on a small table at one end of the hall, the smell of egg pervading the air all evening.

I enjoyed his talks and listened attentively when he told of the Prodigal Son, the Good Samaritan etc, tales I hadn't heard in my own church. His narration was so vivid that I felt as if I was taking part in the past, his mesmerising tone enabling me to forget the drabness of our surroundings. Sometimes he set competitions in the form of questions about the parables he told. On one occasion I received a beautiful book of Bible stories for children for winning one of those competitions. I taunted our Jim all the way home that night as he hadn't won anything. By this time he was getting fed up with dragging me along as he was nearly fifteen, about to leave school and start work, so didn't really want to be bothered by his little sister. When we got home that night he told Mother about our illicit visits. Needless to say our parents forbade us to go there again, and confiscated my book, saying it was "heathen". I just dreaded having to confess to Father O'Keefe about it and prayed to my God that he would be lenient.

When the time came to confess I knew shame such as I had never known before, and the feeling stayed with me for many months afterwards. Father O'Keefe sighed heavily, and his voice thick with sorrow he said "I can only hope you have learned something from this, Mary. We each have our own religion and God must have been sad to know, if only for a little while, you chose to go elsewhere". My penance was very long that day.

One day a new priest came to our church, I can't now remember his name, only that he was very slim, with blonde hair flopping over his eyes and the loveliest smile I had ever seen. All the girls fell in love with him, but none of us confessed to this. Each time he walked by a hint of mothballs tickled my nostrils, corroding the wonderful romantic image I held in my heart.

Sometimes his clean-shaven face would colour in embarrassment as he caught the adoring gazes of a dozen or so adolescent girls, gazing open-mouthed at him, and I felt his confusion. Father O'Keefe was amazed at how keen we all were to attend the Sunday School, which we had sadly neglected for many long months, but wisely kept his own counsel. I remember how guilty I felt during one Sunday Mass when he thanked God for showing the children of the congregation the way to the Light in attending the Sunday

School. The young Priest left as suddenly as he had arrived, and slowly the attendance at Sunday School diminished until only the boys were left.

Since those days I have attended services, christenings, weddings and funerals at churches of differing denominations, but none of them ever gave me the same, wonderful feeling of piety that the Holy Family Church and its Fathers blessed me with for the first sixteen years of my life.

CHAPTER
TEN

Life's Little Accidents

Six children,
numerous ailments,
various broken bones,
all mended
with a smile,
a kiss,
and a cup
of
hot chocolate!

Trials and Tribulations

It was just as well medical treatment was totally free in those days as I don't know how my parents would have coped!

Denis broke both his legs, first one then the other, playing football and seemed to spend most of his time in plaster when I was growing up! I can remember scribbling on his plaster cast with crayons, and he also got a couple of autographs from some Blues players! He kept the one cast for years. He also broke his arm when he fell off the slide in the park. Jimmy fell under the wheels of a car, in Cattell Road, and was rushed off to the "Acci" (Accident Hospital), where they rejoined the skin of his ankle to the rest of his foot. He also had the misfortune to be stricken by a non-fatal strain of meningitis, but luckily, thanks to the skill of the doctors, suffered no lasting effects.

Chris, my then youngest sister, got knocked down on the Coventry Road, just outside the police station, hobbled in to the sergeant and said "I think I've broken my nose!". She certainly had and those wonderful policemen took her to the Accident Hospital, first stopping off to collect my Mother from the house.

I wasn't really accident-prone, just unlucky in that I'd been born with a "spot" (something to do with T.B. I think) on my lung, which meant many years of sun-ray treatment at the local school clinic. Before this I was taken into a convalescent home, I think it was somewhere in Wales but, as I was only about four at the time my memory of the exact place is hazy.

On arrival there, our journey in a big black car quite exciting for me, I was whisked off through a big wooden gate, carried (as I hadn't the energy to walk at that time) through the most beautiful gardens, the scent of roses drifting on the air, into a huge white building. A long verandah ran all around the perimeter, its green painted roof giving shade from the hot sun. Funny-shaped chairs, long basket-weave bodies with black frames and wheels, rested along its length. Little did I realise that I would be spending a lot of time in one of those in the coming weeks!

My first meal there was boiled fish — I hate fish, it always makes me sick. Despite my screams and cries for my Mother, the nurse in charge tried to spoon-feed me. Temper raised, I knocked the spoon out of her hands and tried to run away. She caught me quite easily and carried me back to my seat, this was one of those with a hole in the centre for a "Potty". As I was sat, quite heavily, into the chair, the little round section which concealed the potty when it was in place, fell out and my bottom got stuck in the hole! My screams, I am sure, could be heard for miles around.

At night they used to wake us up with a tin cup filled with hot milk — ugh! Mine always had the skin on it and smelled sour to me.

My first walk with them, some three weeks or so after my admittance, was down a country lane and I stopped every few minutes to admire the flowers, the grass, cows in the field, anything and everything, as it was all quite new to me. I can still remember the wonderful country smells of new-mown hay, wild flowers, strawberries growing in abundance, and another, less-pleasant aroma — I now know it was manure!

Returning home, "fat and full of life" my Mother says, I began my sun ray treatment. It involved me sitting in front of a sort of sun lamp, dark glasses on my eyes, bare chest exposed to the delicious heat. After a few minutes, a Nurse would come in, turn me round and repeat the exercise on my back. As the years rolled on I resented the weekly trips to the Clinic and, at the age of 15, decided I wasn't going any more! Luckily I now enjoy good health but wish I had been blessed with it when I was young.

We used to go to the same clinic for our dental treatment and I hated the smell of the gas they used in those days. I would heave before I even reached the door of the surgery! One lovely summer day I had a tooth extracted and came round to find I was hanging over the windowsill of the room, my head practically inside a bush outside the window. Apparently I had panicked when they gave me the anaesthetic and took too deep a breath!

Mother needed to go the dentist one day as her gums were sore and, sometimes, bled. I went along with her as moral support. The dentist was housed in an old bank building on the corner of Regent Park Road. My Mother was smiling when she went in, but crying when she came out. All her bottom teeth had been removed as she had a gum disease which meant all her teeth would, eventually, fall out. Worse was to come, she was to go back the next week for the top set to be removed. That was bad enough, but she then had to wait nearly six weeks for a set of dentures. It must have been awful for her, she was only about thirty-six at the time and a very beautiful-looking woman.

A couple of weeks after she had received her new teeth we were shopping, on the Coventry Road, when she suddenly sneezed, clapped one hand to her mouth and said "Oh, Mary, my teeth!". Puzzled I followed her gaze — a few feet away from the kerb, on the road, was Mother's top set! Just as I rushed to pick them up a bus came along and ran over them. As soon as the bus had gone I knelt down and retrieved what was left of her teeth — a few bits of enamel! Luckily the dentist was open and said her new teeth would be with him in just a couple of weeks. I don't think he believed us when we told him what had happened to the first set!

I still can't stand the smell of a dentist's surgery to this day, even though they don't use the awful gas anymore. As soon as I step inside that is all I can smell.

I had been suffering with a "grumbling" appendix for a couple of years when one day, whilst crossing the lane on my way to Little Green Lane Junior School, I collapsed in pain just as a solitary car drove up the lane. The car driver who had pulled up in time, took me to school and explained what had happened to my teacher. The next thing I knew I was ensconced in the head-master's car and taken home, there to await the visit from the doctor.

The doctor decided I needed an operation so arranged for the ambulance to come as soon as possible. My heart dropped, it was December 8th and I was worried that I wouldn't be home in time for Christmas. The thought of an operation didn't bother me in the slightest. I had spent so many hours in the Children's Hospital whilst growing up, I was immune to any fears.

Lying on the narrow bed in the ambulance, Mother's pretty face wearing a worried frown, I mulled over the possibilities of being an invalid for a while. All my friends from school would come and visit, bringing sweets and things to cheer me up; I would get special attention from my Mother, for if ever we were ill she always cooked nice little treats, a soft-boiled egg (a luxury for us), with thin, best-buttered "soldiers" of bread, lovely milky drinks of Horlicks, delicious Ribena — the list was endless and I lay back, sighing.

Once inside the hospital I lay quietly whilst a nurse painted my stomach, explaining it was so the surgeon could see where he would be doing the operation! The operation was scheduled for the next morning and I went to sleep that night eager for morning to come!

I was in a small two-bed ward at the end of a large ward. On my first night there I was the only occupant, but a nurse told me a boy named Mervyn was in the recovery room and would be joining me the following day. He, too, had had his appendix out.

Due to an emergency my operation was cancelled and I finally had my appendix out on 11th December, which was also my Father's birthday. I felt groggy when I came round in the Recovery Room, asked for a drink of water; they only allowed me a little sip, and I was promptly sick! I started to realise then that the cosy little picture I'd created for myself was far from reality.

The big ward had wonderful smells, some came from

the polish spread on the floor by big, buffer-type machines, others from the covered dishes containing our meals and some from the clinically clean toilets. Added to this was the smell of cold, winter air carried in on the clothes of the visitors, and I loved them all.

The excitement reached fever-pitch in the wards as Christmas Day approached and, although I felt sad that I wouldn't be with my family for the big day, another part of me was longing to experience something different. A huge tree, carried in by one of the porters, took pride of place at the end of the ward and the children who were well enough were allowed to assist in decorating it. Gift-wrapped parcels appeared almost overnight to sit serenely under the gorgeous tree, and the Nurses went about humming snatches of Christmas carols. I was enthralled by every sight, sound and smell and couldn't wait for Christmas morning.

Two nights before Christmas Day, too excited to sleep, I turned over to face Mervyn's bed and got the fright of my life. He was lying, unmoving, his eyes wide open, staring at me. Quietly I called his name but received no reply. Slipping out of bed I walked round to his, touched his shoulder and called him again, still no reply. Terrified I ran out into the big ward to the Night Sister at the entrance. Keeping my voice as low as possible I said "I think you'd better come and look at Mervyn, Nurse, I think he's dead!". Rising rapidly to her feet she walked briskly down the length of the ward, her rubber-soles shoes making a kind of hissing sound as they made contact with the polished floor. Motioning me to remain outside our room she approached the still form

101

of Mervyn. A couple of minutes later, a smile playing at the corner of her mouth, she said "It's all right, Mary dear, he sleeps with his eyes open!". I clapped a hand to my mouth and whispered "He said he's going to marry me when we grow up. I can't marry someone who sleeps with his eyes open!". The nurse turned away, her slim shoulders shaking with laughter as she walked back down the ward.

On Christmas Eve I was told I was going home and I was devastated. I pleaded with the doctor to let me stay there for Christmas but to no avail. However, there were compensations, a beautiful watch, a small battery-operated radio, (luxury indeed!), sweets galore, fruit, books and pencils filled my stocking on Christmas morning. How my parents managed to afford all those things I just don't know, but they made one little girl very happy. So it was worth being ill after all and I had a wonderful scar to show all my friends when I went back to school!

Looking back I would imagine my family must have used up all Dad's insurance contributions, plus perhaps quite a bit of lots of other working-class people, on the excellent care we all received from the N.H.S.

CHAPTER
ELEVEN

Heroes and Heroines

Alan Ladd, Cary Grant,
"big" John Wayne,
cowboys, or swashbucklers
on the Spanish Main.
Maureen O'Hara, Doris Day,
super Sophia Loren —
whatever the scenario
they always got their men!
James Cagney, Clark Gable,
lovely Stewart Granger,
all fought courageously,
living for the danger!
Richard Burton, John Mills,
lovely Marilyn Monroe,
Rock Hudson, Glen Ford,
we loved them so!
Sixpence was all it cost
to enjoy every scene
of their adventures
on the Silver Screen!

The Silver Screen

Mother loved the cinema and quite often cajoled us into playing "hooky" from school so we could accompany her. Although I moaned and groaned a lot about losing time from school, it was really just a gesture as I, too, loved the "flicks".

On these afternoon excursions Mother sailed forth, the newest baby tucked up in the pushchair, her bottle of milk wrapped in a couple of napkins to keep it warm, a bottle of cold tea, pieces of bread and jam, or bread and dripping, and always a handful of Bluebird chocolate-covered caramel toffees which she divided equally during the interval, placed in the tartan shopping bag. For a couple of hours we were lost in the magic taking place on the screen, sighing when the lights finally went up and the curtains closed.

We were lucky enough to have three cinemas in Small Heath, the Grange, the Coronet and the Kingston. My favourite was the Coronet, which sat proudly on the Coventry Road, its wide, marble-like steps stretching the width of the building. As I climbed these I often imagined I was a film star attending the premier of my latest, world-renowned film, wearing a long, shimmering evening gown, a handsome escort ready to pander to my every whim (especially with regard to huge boxes of delicious chocolates!), holding my elbow. This feeling was intensified if we could afford to sit upstairs!

The interior of the Coronet was opulent, from the plush seats, the thickly-carpeted aisles and the smart uniforms of the usherettes, to the swish of the heavy, ornate curtains covering the screen. The scent of bees-wax polish lingered in the air, until the adults lit up their cigarettes! When an usherette passed by I pictured myself, a few years hence, dressed in a smart uniform, brass buttons gleaming, neat pillbox hat perched jauntily on my head, smiling and showing the patrons to their seats. One particular usherette, tall, slim, and very pretty, always smelled of Palmolive soap, adding to the pleasure in my surroundings.

My head was filled with beauty, not only of the heroines of the day, Elizabeth Taylor, Doris Day and Lana Turner, but also with the opulence of my surround-ings. I revelled in the warmth and comfort of that particular cinema. The heroes, Rock Hudson, Cary Grant and the swashbuckling Stewart Granger filled my girlhood dreams. When we related details of the films we had seen to the other children, their faces would be green with envy as, whilst we had been enjoying ourselves, they had been stuck in a chalky classroom struggling with maths or some other boring subject!

Sometimes, during our Talent Shows, we acted out some of the scenes we had witnessed in whatever film we had seen that particular week, to the envy of all the other children. Of course they never knew if we were portraying the drama correctly, not having been lucky enough to have actually seen the film.

The Grange cinema, much smaller and less imposing than the Coronet, nestled on the corner of Grange Road and Coventry Road, opposite Maturi's lawnmower shop. Its curved steps struggled to contain excitable young bodies on Saturday mornings. For just sixpence (less than three new pence) we enjoyed the adventures of Flash Gordon, the Lone Ranger, etc. The noise was deafening, not from the characters on screen but from the boys. Every boy in those days was either Tonto, or the Lone Ranger, many of them arriving at the cinema wearing home-made black masks and carrying toy guns, which the Manager confiscated until they were going home. Some of them raced around, shouting at the tops of their voices, until a quick cuff round the ear from the Manager or staff curtailed their exuberance.

On quite a few occasions there were so many children waiting in the queue that the Manager had to turn half of us away, telling us to come back the next week. Our disappointment was tangible, made worse by the smug looks and snide comments of the lucky ones. No matter what we did to fill those few hours while our contemporaries were ensconced in the magic, the joy disappeared from our play. As soon as the morning matinée was over groups of us gathered around the various yards and street corners to listen, enthralled, as the entire programme, including the forthcoming attractions, was related to us by our friends.

I loved the Pathé News and the "trailers", which whetted our appetites for the coming weeks. I also loved the smell of the plush seats, deep burgundy in colour with highly-polished, but scarred, arms. The wonderful aroma of choc ices, not always affordable, waited under our noses as the usherettes walked by, together with the sweet, sticky smell of popcorn. Without these treats our enjoyment of the film was dulled a little.

The one smell I couldn't stand was whatever they used

to clean the ladies' toilets. These were approached by a downward flight of slightly curved, dark red pitted stone steps, and before I'd even reached the bottom and the heavy door which would take me into the loos, the smell assaulted me. My nostrils twitched with the desire to sneeze and tears filled my eyes, as I tried, in vain, not to.

Off-white stone sinks lined one wall, mottled mirrors above, one small window set high in the wall, covered with a piece of wire mesh, allowed distorted daylight to seep in. We didn't linger in there, the smell was far too overpowering, the strong bleach-like stench sending us scurrying back to the welcome smells of the auditorium in double-quick time.

The Grange seemed to me like a friend, well-loved, warm and welcoming and I was loathe to leave its comforts.

The Kingston, majestically placed on the top of Kingston Hill, lay back from the road, it's off-white frontage gleaming brightly on sunny days, acting like a beacon to us all. Jim worked there for a while as a Junior Projectionist and was sometimes given concessionary tickets, which he passed on to us. Sometimes we were allowed to use these tickets to sit in the "Gods" — the upper balcony, and I always felt rich and important on these occasions.

Most of the seats in the back row of the balcony were used by courting couples and I watched, open-mouthed, at some of the antics they got up to. As I grew into adolescence I longed for the day when I too could sit in the back row, away from the madness of the stalls, with my true love. I promised myself I would not kiss him with a mouth full of the sticky, pink, smelly chewing gum that most of the other girls seemed to enjoy when kissing their boyfriends.

When I finally did meet the man of my dreams, some two years later, we went to the Futurist cinema to see *Quatermass Experiment*, which frightened me so much, I was unable to enjoy the romantic atmosphere of the back row in the gallery!

A new X-rated film came out entitled *"The Blob"*, which my Mother dearly wanted to see. Father only liked western films so suggested she take me along. I was terrified. Apart from the fact that even though at fourteen I was too young to see an X-film, I only looked about eleven. Undeterred, my Mother dressed me up; a pair of her old grey court shoes, stuffed with papers so they fit better, a bright green pac-a-mac, tucked up around my waist and held in place with the belt, tied so tightly I could hardly breathe, and the top of a nylon stocking would round my head with my hair tucked into it. The finishing touches were applied, some "vanishing" powder on my face, cyclamen lipstick, some of it rubbed into my cheeks to give them colour, smeared on my lips and I was ready. When I looked into the mirror I was horrified, I looked about forty years old!

Ignoring my pleas, Mother sailed out of the house with me tottering along in her wake. I received many strange looks from passers-by and muttering furiously to myself, allowed Mother to urge me on. On reaching the Coronet I hugged the wall as the queue shuffled slowly forward, dreading the moment when the bright lights of the foyer would surely show me up for the fraud I was.

When we reached the top of the steps Mother hissed "Don't look up, don't speak, just walk!". A sudden push in my back from Mother had me practically falling into the darkened cinema and I grabbed at the first solid thing I touched. In the semi-darkness I couldn't tell what I had grabbed hold of, until a voice said "Are you all right, Madam?". Blushing furiously and grateful for the covering darkness, I mumbled something and shuffled to my seat, the eagle eye of the Manager boring into my back I slid down as low as possible into my seat, keeping my eyes downcast, praying he wouldn't decide to take another look at "Madam".

For me the whole evening was a disaster, especially when the Manager kept walking up and down the aisle by me, casting quizzical looks in my direction. Even worse was Mother telling me to go to the toilet before the lights went up for the interval, warning me to stay in there until I heard the opening music for the next half. I can't repeat some of the things that were said to me as I stumbled over feet, bags and coats as I groped my way to the toilets. I was so glad when the film was over and we could go home.

As we walked, slowly, home, necessitated because the scrunched up newspaper had hardened and Mother's shoes were killing me, a dark figure stepped out of a shop doorway, said something we didn't quite catch and started to walk alongside us. Mother suddenly sprinted away and I had no option but to follow suit. Halfway along the Coventry Road I stopped to take off the cumbersome shoes and ran the rest of the way barefoot, conscious all the time of the quickening footsteps of the stranger. We reached the comparative safety of our entry and stopped to gather our breath. My heart froze when I saw the stranger rapidly approaching us. Grabbing my Mother's arm, I hissed "He's here, Mum, that man's here". As if accepting our fate she whispered "When I tell you run up and fetch your Father, don't worry about me, I'll trip him up! Before I could move, a peppermint-flavoured mist lingered near my cheek, followed by a deep, rich voice saying "Goodnight, ladies!" and the stranger walked on. Trying hard not to break into hysterical laughter, Mother said, "Oh, the Lord bless us! It was only Mr Essex after all!".

My blistered feet were a painful reminder of that evening for many days to come, and the worst thing of all as far as I was concerned was that I didn't even enjoy the film, it had frightened me to death!

When I was fourteen and Jim was seventeen we were invited to be Godparents to my cousin, Margaret's, first son. After a lot of discussion it was agreed by our parents that we were quite old enough to travel to Luton in Bedfordshire on our own for the christening. On the Saturday evening prior to the event, we went, with our younger cousins, to the local cinema to see *The Young Ones*, starring my idol, Cliff Richard.

The atmosphere inside the cinema was electric, pulsating with bopping, rocking teddy-boys, hair slicked into enormous quiffs with Brylcreem, the smell of which was nauseating! Stick-thin legs in drain-pipe trousers twitched and shivered to the beat of the title song. Girls, hair either tied up in pony tails, or piled into impossible heights atop their heads, full skirts over many-tiered rainbow coloured underskirts, drenched in Tweed perfume, its musky smell, wonderful in small doses, causing my eyes to water and my nose to twitch with a desire to sneeze, danced on the seats, in the aisles, some grabbing the boys arms and being thrown over their shoulders, and under their legs, screaming with joy. Chewing-gum filled jaws moved in time to the rhythm, some even managing to blow sickly-scented bubbles at the same time! A kaleidoscope of colour filled my head and, so caught up was I in the exuberance of my contemporaries, it was many minutes before we realised the music had ceased.

Silence descended, the couples froze as if turned to stone, their limbs captured in half-movement, eyes glittering. The Manager, flanked by two tall, well-built young men, stood nervously on the stage in front of the house curtain. His small, rotund body quivered, waist-coat buttons threatening to explode at any moment as his chest heaved, red carnation wilting rapidly in his button-hole, as he cast fearful glances at the suddenly alien crowd.

In a tone reminiscent of Winston Churchill, he warned us to sit down or he would cancel the film. Within minutes there was a mad scramble for the seats and, sweating profusely, the Manager and his aides stepped down from the stage, slipping through a side door to avoid coming into contact with any of his patrons.

As soon as the curtains opened the entire audience broke into song, and continued to sing, clap and cheer throughout the entire film, but the Manager never reappeared!

That evening was the most exhilarating of my life at that time and, even today, when I catch a hint of Tweed "eau de parfum", I am transported to that wonderful event.

I once went out with a boy from my office and, because he didn't live in Birmingham, asked me to direct us from the top of Hill Street, by the old GPO building where we'd arranged to meet, to the Gaumont cinema in the city centre. Geography had never been my strong point at school and, after walking around in the rain for a couple of hours, we ended up in a side street outside The Gaiety cinema, some way distant from the Gaumont!

He approached the pay desk, eyes glittering with anger, and purchased one ticket. I only had about three shillings (approximately fifteen pence) in my purse, some of which was my bus-fare home. Unwilling to invoke his terrible temper, having witnessed it at work, I duly paid for my own ticket, then followed his retreating back. The film was something to do with a man coming out of a fog, which really added to the overall depression which had settled over me, not helped by the damp and smoky atmosphere of the auditorium. On top of this his first words of greeting resounded in my brain: "What have you done to your hair?" In those days my hair was very long and straight but, wishing to appear a bit sophisticated for my first date with him, I had been to the hairdresser that morning and had it set in the beehive style, so popular then, to give me some height. He was six feet two inches to my five feet two inches, so I needed all the help I could get. Obviously, in his eyes,

I'd failed. I knew our relationship was over before it had really begun when he offered me a cigarette, a Gold Leaf, then broke it in half and gave me the half with the tip! I did go out with him a couple of times after that, but that's another story.

I have since visited cinemas in different towns but none of them had the majesty of the Kingston, the grandeur of the Coronet or the homeliness of the Grange. One thing they all have in common is the smell, that hasn't changed a bit!

CHAPTER
TWELVE

Pictures in the Fire

Creatures dancing
in leaping flames,
giant horses
with flowing manes,
devils, elves
and little folk —
disappearing
in puffs of smoke.

Rivers, streams
and mountains tall
casting shadows
on the wall,
forest glades
and seashores wild,
bringing magic
to a child.

Heat

When our Jim started work I inherited the task of going to Tranter's coal-yard on Green Lane for our coal. Pushing the home-made barrow along the cobbled lane I prayed I wouldn't meet any of my school-friends, but invariably did. Blushing furiously I would hold my head up high, straighten my shoulders and stalk off down the lane. The barrow only held one hundredweight of coal, which cost just ten shillings (fifty new pence), so if we were purchasing two hundredweight I had to make two journeys to that awful place. Sometimes we could only afford a few shillingsworth of nutty slack, which was the odd bits and dregs from the bottom of the huge, glistening heaps of shiny black coal. Not only did it smell evil to me, it looked and felt it as our fingers would be sore for days after scooping it up once we got home.

The pungent, dust-laden air of the coal-yard caused my throat to itch and its smell to linger in my nostrils from Saturday to Saturday. Many yards from the gates of my own personal Hell the odour would assail me, conjuring up pictures of weary pit ponies dragging heavy carts of coal deep in the bowels of the earth, never seeing daylight. I worried about the men who toiled so far below us and imagined the injuries they sustained, ominous slag-heaps overshadowing once pretty villages and the children, grimy and sad. I loved the warmth the coal gave us but hated the suffering it surely caused to those who provided it. Some years later my deep-seated fears became a tragic reality with the disaster of Aberfan.

On my return from the coal-yard Mother, Theresa and myself would painstakingly empty the barrow, shovelful by shovelful, into the little coalhole. On the occasions when we did buy two hundredweight, I would simply tip up the barrow onto the cobbles outside the kitchen window, leave the rest of them to shovel it up and then trek back to the coal-yard once more. My God must have been heartily sick of my prayers for deliverance from that task!

How I wished we could be like the other families in the yard and have our coal delivered, but as Wednesday was delivery day we could never afford it, having to wait until Saturday when Mother received Dad's wages. The big, muscled coal-man would stomp up the yard, his hob-nailed boots ringing on the cobbles, as he delivered his load. He would struggle through the narrow doorway of Mrs H's house, that good lady having removed all her mats and placed newspaper down before she'd allow him inside the door, and deposit the coal in the little coalhole tucked by the side of the stairs in the kitchen.

The soot which gathered in the chimney was put to good use in our house, a bit of it smeared onto a tooth-brush with a pinch of bicarbonate of soda added made a wonderful, if gritty, toothpaste! My family's teeth were as white as snow, and years later a dentist told me he had never seen such white teeth, but cast me a disparaging look when I told him of our home-made toothpaste.

Sometimes, if the weather was very cold and finances allowed, Mother would light the fire in the bedroom and I would be the first to climb into the comfort of the big bed, after it had first been warmed with a milk bottle filled with hot water then wrapped in a piece of sheeting. Sometimes a house brick was warmed in the ovens of the fire, wrapped in newspaper, then a piece of calico and tucked under the top sheet. The heat from the brick lasted much longer than that of the milk bottle. Stretching my toes to the very ends of the bed I'd sigh, revelling in the warmth, space and solitude, until my younger sisters dived on me!

When Mum gave birth to Theresa, when I was just three, Father took me round to Mrs H's for the night and I screamed when she put me in bed and jumped out, shouting "There's a thing in the bed!". I can still remember the squashy, sickening feel of the rubber hot water bottle she had placed there for my comfort!

If we hadn't enough money for coal I would push the barrow up to the wood-yard which stood by the betting office at the junction of Coventry Road and Green Lane. Here we could shovel up our own bits of wood and shavings for just a few shillings. It was back-breaking work, and quite frightening as, somehow, the largest pieces of wood were underneath the bench where a wicked-looking, two-edged saw was wielded by a young man. How I never had my ears, or anything else, chopped off as I dodged up and down in time to the rhythm of that saw, I'll never know. I would keep my head as low as possible, blushing quite furiously when I straightened up to see the young man, who was quite handsome, grinning at me.

The smell of the wood was wonderful, some of it reminded me of apples, pine and even, on occasion, when it was burning brightly on our fire, a hint of

Erinmore tobacco would drift into the air, its incredible aroma reminding me forcibly of my Grandfather sitting at the table, sucking on his pipe! My love of the smell of wood has never left me. These days I browse around furniture shops just so I can inhale the delightful aromas of "real" wood.

After many years of black-leading our huge, old-fashioned range in the living room, usually getting more of the black-lead liquid on myself than the range, the Council decided we were to have a new "modern" tiled fire-grate installed. My joy was nothing compared to Mother's. The old fire used so much fuel we burned potato skins, bits of old leather, in fact anything that would burn and save on coal!

On the day the men came to rip out our "monstrosity" we were all thrilled. Fascinated we watched as they first removed the high, wooden mantle-piece covered with a dark red chenille cloth, its tattered fringe evidence of tiny fingers trying to reach the Bluebird chocolate-covered caramels Mother kept up there! The removal of the back-plates revealed smoke-blackened walls and huge gaps in the brickwork. The fire grate and ovens were next, and I sighed when I realised that all the cooking would now be done on the gas stove. I prayed we would have enough pennies for the meter in future! Finally the hearth was removed, and the whole room was enveloped in dust and soot. Coughing and spluttering we all ran outside, Mother included, laughing madly, too eager to see our new fireplace to worry about a bit of dust.

Just a couple of hours after their arrival the workmen

called us back in and, awe-struck, we children gazed in admiration at the new fireplace. Mother didn't seem as enthusiastic and, dragging my eyes away from the fire I could see why. The wallpaper above the fireplace was as black as coal, its lovely floral pattern unrecognisable. Because the old mantle-piece had been quite high, a piece of bare, partially-plastered brickwork stared obscenely at us, at least three foot in height and the same in width. I knew without Mother saying anything, that she was thinking of the cost of re-decorating the entire room! Touching her arm I whispered "There's a sale on in the wallpaper shop on the Cov, Mum. Ann's Mum bought five rolls the other day for just fifteen shillings". At the look on my Mother's face I knew it was out of our reach at the particular time.

Shrugging her shoulders Mother said "Oh, but it is beautiful, it reminds me of the one we had at home!". It was indeed beautiful, its pale cream tiles shone, apart from where bits of cement poked out where the hearth joined the façade of the grate. The hearth sloped gently upwards at the front, its smooth edges affording no danger to the crawling baby of the family. Best of all, its mantle-piece was only about three feet from ground level, so no more would we have to stretch over an open fire to reach whatever we were seeking.

Quickly now Mother shooed us out of the way and bent to lay a fire, scrunching up newspapers, bits of wood, two pieces of a soap-like substance, and finally a few pieces of coal. We waited, and waited, and waited. Mother's pretty face puckered into a frown as she tried again and again to light it. When she started blowing on the pitiful flicker of light she eventually achieved, and started muttering "May all the Saints preserve us" under her breath, we children drifted out into the yard, aware that her patience was on a very short fuse.

Jim looked up at the chimney and remarked that there wasn't any smoke coming out of it. Everyone in the yard gazed upwards, puzzled. Seconds later Mother came running out of the house, her face black with soot, eyes red and watering, streaks of dirt on her clothes, but with a huge smile on her face. "I've done it! I've bested the blighter!" she laughed, and we all followed her back inside to scenes of havoc.

Everything was covered in soot, and lying on the recently-pristine hearth was a large, charred object, unrecognisable to us all. I thought it was a dead bird, but as this would have given the young ones nightmares, I kept my mouth shut. Judging from the smell emanating from it, it certainly wasn't vegetable or mineral! It must have been stuck up in the chimney for years and all the banging by the workmen had dislodged it. In her struggles to get the fire going Mother had, in desperation, pushed the broom up the chimney and brought the disgusting object into the room.

Laughing madly we set to and cleaned up the living room, Mother and ourselves in that order. Denis tried manfully to clean the wallpaper but it simply fell to pieces in his hands. Seeing the sad look on Mother's face he put his arm around her shoulders and said "I'll buy some wallpaper, Mum, and I'll hang it up for you", bringing a smile to her face and a tear to her eye. Denis was working in a shoe warehouse near the city centre and seemed to have loads of money, so Mother knew he could afford it.

By the time Father came home from work the fire was burning brightly, our lovely brass fender gleaming after my strenuous efforts with the Brasso polish, and a delicious meal of curly-kale on the table. We were all far too excited to notice the sooty streaks on the curtains, the top of the chiffonier and piano. It was only when Father commented how dim the gas mantle seemed that we realised it, too, was covered in soot!

Even though all the other people in the yard had modern grates, they came in droves to admire ours. I heard Mother whisper to Mrs H "Sure I only need the electricity now and I'll be a happy woman!". I suddenly realised how hard it was for Mother, but she never complained and always sang as she worked, no matter how tired she was.

Denis duly bought the wallpaper, which I thought was horrible. It had huge, blue flowers on it and made me feel claustrophobic, but Mother loved it. Father bought a rusty brass fireguard from somewhere, which he patiently cleaned until it gleamed, the pungent smell of the polish filling the house. We had never been able to have one round the old black range as we couldn't find one to fit.

I sorely missed the delicious stews, baked apples and potatoes that Mother used to cook on the old range, mainly because the house didn't smell as welcoming any more. Mother agreed that although it was easier to cook these things in the gas oven she too missed the wonderful, enticing aromas that used to drift from our living room and into the yard.

In the depths of winter, ensconced in my father's arm chair, as close to the roaring flames as I could get, cup of weak cocoa clutched in my hand, I never gave a thought to the discomfort I suffered on my weekly trek to the coal-yard. I concentrated instead on the wonderful pictures created by the leaping flames of red, yellow and pale blue and made up stories for my younger sisters. As they grew older they too saw the pictures I had seen, and all because of a bit of coal.

When I was a young mother I too enjoyed the delights of a real, open fire and spent many happy, dark winter afternoons curled up in an armchair, feet on the fender, my first two babies nestled safely in my arms, their faces glowing with joy at the pictures in the flames.

Although I am more than happy to be living in a house with central heating now, I sometimes miss the homely warmth, and the comfort, of the sweet-smelling fires of my childhood, and the opportunity of showing my grandchildren the magical pictures in the flames.

CHAPTER
THIRTEEN

Food For Thought

Byron — moody
Shelley — divine
Shakespeare — favourite.

Dickens — thoughtful
Steinbeck — clever
Wells — haunting.

Delderfield — wonderful
Joyce — keen
Tolstoy — heavy.

A world of words —
for nothing!

The Library

I loved going to the library at the junction of Little Green Lane and Green Lane. My younger sisters thought I was mad for spending so much time in there, they preferred to play in the grimy yard. Leaving them to their childish games I would saunter along the lane, past Wimbush and climb the shiny red steps of the beautiful building which housed my dream-world.

The first thing that struck me was the smell. As I pushed open the heavy glass doors into the reading room, which wasn't really a room more a long corridor-type section at the side of the library proper, the smell of beeswax polish tickled my nostrils.

All the fittings were of wood and brass, the daily newspapers rested, tip-tilted, on a long wooden shelf, which ran the length of the room, their pages held in place by shiny brass arms. It was mostly men who studied the papers, who cast me malevolent looks as I stood on tip-toe pretending to be engrossed in *The Times*, which was way beyond my comprehension then, or our local paper the *Evening Despatch*. Sometimes I tried to sneak at look at the *News of the World*, forbidden at home. I never got beyond the first page as the librarian, her leather-soled shoes squeaking on the highly-polished wooden floor, deftly removed it from under my nose! Sniffing loudly she bundled the offending paper under her arm, muttering "I don't know how that got there!". I often thought she read it when no-one else was looking!

One elderly man grunting and shuffling always came

to hover at my elbow, hissing "When you've quite finished, lassie!". As I walked away I heard him rustling the pages back into their pristine condition.

I savoured the walk through the narrow passage by the librarian's desk, willing myself not to run and throw myself into my favourite place. Once through there and into the library itself I was enthralled. Shelves and shelves of books soared high into the air, the green light from the glass-domed roof highlighting the gold lettering on some of the classics. I always ignored the children's section, heading straight for the adult books. Because I usually collected books for Denis, who was three years older than me, I was allowed to borrow books from that section on his ticket. I longed for the day when I too would be adult and could choose grown-up books on my own ticket.

What the librarian thought of Denis' literary choice was clearly written all over her face, as she stamped books such as *"Gone with the Wind"*, *"How Green was my Valley"*, along with books on sport and fishing! Sometimes I'd pinch our Jim's ticket as well, staggering home with my precious load.

Tables, and chairs with seats of dark red leather, highly polished and creaky, were placed at strategic points around this section and I loved nothing more than to choose a book then sit down, head bent in rapture. On one occasion I decided to read *War and Peace*, having spent many long hours in the library to do so as it was far too heavy for me to carry home. On finally finishing, it two years after I'd started, I am ashamed to admit I didn't understand a word of it, but it was a task I had set

125

myself so had to see it through to the end. I was only about thirteen at the time!

Each time I opened a book it was like opening a surprise parcel — and the joy of finding what was inside overwhelmed me on occasion. For me, at that time, the smell of books could not be surpassed by anything else. Some smelled of old leather, parchment paper and ink. The newer books had a crisp, no-nonsense sort of smell, but it was the old books I loved best. It wasn't just the smell, it was also the feel, especially the old ones, their covers were warm to the touch, well-thumbed and, obviously, well-loved. I couldn't wait to be grown up and promised myself I would have a library of my very own then. I envied the smart librarians and hoped, one day, to be lucky enough to work in such a wonderful environment.

I pictured myself in a neat, dark blue shirt-waist dress, slim leather belt at my waist, hair pulled back into a tidy chignon, and spectacles perched daintily on my nose! From my lofty seat behind the high counter all the borrowers would clamour for my literary knowledge, and smiling I would comply.

I was amazed at the items previous borrowers left inside the books. There was usually the odd bus ticket, cleaning tickets, sometimes a piece of string, or a hair ribbon. Those items were, I believed, used as book marks. Occasionally a proper bookmark or a photograph would be enfolded in the pages. These latter items I always handed to the librarian.

On opening a copy of Jane Austen's *Pride and Prejudice* one evening, relaxed in the chair, the evening sunlight casting a mellow green shadow over my head, I was delighted to find a pressed, pure-white, rose petal in its hallowed pages. The edges were slightly furled, obviously someone had closed the book very clumsily. In my imagination I saw a young woman receiving a beautiful bouquet of these flowers, smelling their wonderful fragrance before placing them in a vase, retaining just one which she slipped into the pages of the book. My imagination ran on, were they from her one true love I wondered, or were they part of her bridal bouquet? Perhaps she had been ill, and they were a gift from someone dear to her. The bell tolling closing time, eerie in that wonderful silence so peculiar to that library, had me rising slowly to my feet, still wrapped in my thoughts.

The strangest item, wrapped in a piece of foil paper in the centre pages of an historical novel, puzzles me still. It was a card containing four, tiny pearly buttons, the sort used on knitted baby garments, matinee-coats etc.

On lifting the card to my face a soft wisp of some kind of powder drifted under my nose, gentle, delicate. Why were they inside the book? Had the lady, for I was sure it was a lady, been knitting with the book open on her lap, been disturbed — perhaps by her baby — and just popped the buttons inside? Perhaps, my imagination really took hold now, the baby had died and the buttons were no longer needed. My Mother had, quite recently, suffered the loss of a newborn baby boy and, as soon as she came home from the hospital, had put all the tiny knitted garments, some unfinished, away. Tears fell down my cheeks when I likened the previous reader of the book to my Mother, and sadly I put it back on the shelf and went home. Perhaps, one day when things were better, I thought, the lady would come back and retrieve the book and its contents.

The worst thing I ever found was a small, smelly piece of fish, squashed into the centre pages of a book about fly-fishing, which Denis had asked me to collect for him. I dread to think what the previous borrower had been doing and can remember carrying that book home at arm's length, receiving very strange looks from passers-by!

On leaving that wonderful building I strolled down the lane, my arms clasped around books, pretending I was a college student on the verge of an interesting career, or discovery. The books felt alive in my arms and I couldn't wait to get home to discover their secrets.

The peace and quiet I found in the library was bliss! Our little house, crammed to bursting with bodies, and very noisy most of the time, wasn't the ideal place to concentrate on anything, especially the magic of words. If Mother didn't need me to go to the shops, I could guarantee she would want me to look after my sisters while she got on with something else. When I went to bed each night, usually early so I could read my book before the last of the daylight crept into the room, my sisters were often still awake and begged me to tell them stories.

Each night we lay in the big double bed, its foot-board resting against the outer edge of the foot-board on my parents bed, the baby's cot at the end of our bed, cuddling close together for warmth under thin blankets and Gran's old fur coat, as I told them tales of fairies, witches, the creatures in the cut and princesses. All my stories had happy endings as I didn't want my little sisters to have nightmares. Apart from that, of course, Mother would have killed me if they did!

I also loved the school library, a large room filled from floor to ceiling with books. A large, round table dominated the centre of the room, straight-backed chairs, so comfortable, resting around its edges. Unlike some of my classmates I was more than happy to browse around in there, trying to absorb the knowledge those books offered. The room always smelled as if it had been freshly cleaned with some kind of floral substance. It was, to me, a haven of peace away from the hustle and bustle of the school just beyond its brown painted and glass door.

Shakespeare has been my favourite author since I was thirteen years old, conjuring up an entirely different world, one of beauty but also one of fear and history. His "mercy" speech in *The Merchant of Venice* remains in my mind and I was so envious when another girl was given the part of Portia in the school production of that play. I had to be content with the role of Jessica, Shylock's daughter, whose limited speech left a lot to be desired, I thought then.

I was fortunate in being given a complete Works of Shakespeare, First Edition. The beautiful deep red, soft tooled leather was a joy, the flimsy gold-edged pages warm to the touch, and the smell was wonderful. Unfortunately my youngest sister, Jean, at the age of three had no idea of the beauty of books and destroyed them with her coloured pencils! I was absolutely devastated on returning home to find pages of my precious Works scattered around the bedroom, in the living room and under the cushions! In her own way she has since made amends — by presenting me many years later with another complete Works, although not first edition or soft leather, but welcome just the same.

For our English Literature, "O" level exam we read *The History of Mr Polly* by H. G. Wells. My heart wept for the poor, downtrodden Mr Polly and rejoiced when he took off on his own. Lying in bed, reading by the mellow glare of the flickering gaslight, I became engrossed in his many problems, most of which I felt then were caused because he appeared to be a weak-willed man. I was so relieved when it all turned out fine for him in the end!

My Father and my English Teacher, Mrs Watts, always encouraged me to read, Father saying it was food for the brain. Mother often said I would go blind as I had my head stuck in a book so often, especially when she needed me to do something for her.

I always felt very clever after a visit to the library — I don't know why, unless it's because I had time, and space, to absorb everything I read there. Not many of my school-friends were such avid readers as myself, so I couldn't discuss my latest reading matter with them. They appeared to be more interested in television, which we didn't have as we had gas lighting, records and make-up. I did once try to discuss one of Shakespeare's plays with a school-friend and she astounded me by asking "What number is that in the Hit Parade". I think the Bard would have chuckled to think that *Romeo and Juliet* were rated number one!

Books were a source of joy and stimulation to me, and have remained so ever since. Nothing gave me greater pleasure on dark, winter evenings, the leaping flames from the fire casting shadows on the walls, the little radio, tuned in to Mother's favourite programme, playing softly in the background, the tantalising smell of tomorrow's stew filtering through the air and all my siblings out of sight, than to curl up in my Father's old armchair and lose myself in the wonderful world portrayed in the pages before me.

On warm summer days I sat on our doorstep, nose in a book, oblivious to the noise of the inhabitants of the yard. The adults used to smile and say "she's clever is your Mary", and Mother, casting me an exasperated look, muttered "Sure, that child wouldn't know if a bomb fell on her!".

Returning from the library one foggy, autumn evening, my eyes trying to scan the first few pages of my latest book, I walked straight into a lamp-post, curing me immediately of that particular habit!

On entering my local library today, totally different in every way to the one of my childhood, apart from the smell, I still feel just as excited and over-awed as I did on my visits during those wonderful, halcyon days of my early teenage years.

CHAPTER
FOURTEEN

Today in Small Heath Park

I walked around, shocked and dismayed,
to see the changes where I once played.
Gone are the pools, gone too the green
where elderly bowlers were always seen.

The slides and swings, now yellow and red,
locked behind fencing where dogs dare not tread.
Magical lily pond, long disappeared,
scene of our fantasies for so many years.

The rustic bridge, a beautiful sight,
seemed to go missing — almost overnight
No more tennis courts, instead a ball park
where lots of youths were having a "lark".

No more the boating lake, but swans swim serene
in the once crystal waters, now coloured green.
Gone are the flower beds, gone too the trees,
can someone tell me — what's happened to these?

The refreshment hut once proud on a hill,
no longer is there our stomachs to fill

with delicious flavours of lovely ice-cream
Looking back, it all seems a dream.

Shocked by the changes in just a few years
I couldn't stem my flood-tide of tears.
From inside this spectacle I stood and stared,
wishing that someone, somewhere, still cared.

Victoria Park
(Commonly known as Small Heath Park)

As children we didn't appreciate the beautiful flower displays that abounded in the park. The park-keeper and gardeners spent many hours creating, maintaining and watering the different scenes. Sometimes, as on "royal" occasions there were the most incredible displays, all ignored as we raced past them to the swings. The gorgeous scents of roses, tulips, daffodils and the like escaped us then. Their beauty didn't hold a candle to the magic world of the paddling pool, slides, roundabouts etc, and the secret nooks and crannies we used as our hideaways.

The helter-skelter was my eldest brother Denis's favourite until the day he fell off and broke his arm! The witch's hat, a cone shaped structure with long metal arms, resembling spiders' legs, protruding from the roof, so supporting the wooden seat around the circumference, was my particular favourite. Whilst I swung round and round on this, sometimes being daring enough to stand on the wooden platform, I dreamed of the day I would meet my handsome Prince, who would, of course, carry me off to his castle high in the hills and give me everything my heart desired for the rest of my life.

I can still remember the wonderful, free feeling I had when I rose higher and higher on the swings, stretching my toes out as far as they would go, sometimes even managing to touch the upper-most branches of the trees. My head was filled with thoughts of the future, and I longed for a place where I could be as free as when I was on those swings.

On entering the park from its main entrance on the Coventry Road, we raced madly past the park-keeper's house, a beautiful building and one I would have loved to explore, past the Sons of Rest building, and the "sons" relaxing on benches lining the route, taking a well-earned rest from their soldiering days. On and on we ran, beyond the bowling green, up past the beautiful floral displays, to get to the "refreshment rooms", perched on a small hill. Sitting outside on the wooden benches, under cover of an overhanging canopy, licking delicious Walls ice-creams, and watching the swans gliding around on the lake a few feet below us was like being in another world. It was so peaceful there, away from the noise of the paddling pools.

Once down by the lake itself we missed completely the beauty of its small islands and the families of ducks waddling along the edge, concentrating instead on children pushing out paper boats, which rapidly disintegrated. Sometimes, to the envy of us all, a "posh" family appeared, the father proudly carrying a motorised boat which his offspring very rarely touched. Sometimes one of our crowd would be dared to swim across the lake, but a quick cuff rom the ever-vigilant keeper prevented this foolhardy action.

Hidden away in the dark recesses of the park, overhung by huge age-old trees, was the lily pond, spanned by a rustic bridge. With fearful trepidation we dared each other to run across the bridge, ever watchful for the sight of any "little people", whom we were told lived in the mud at the base of the bridge. We often came upon courting couples, who jumped visibly as we careered across the bridge. Huge lilies covered the surface of the dark green water, which smelled obnoxious, making me imagine all kinds of horrible things lurking under the water.

Our ideal place was the paddling pool. Originally there was just one large pool, quite shallow and very boring. Someone then decided that two further pools should be built, with the added attraction of a ship in the centre one. We couldn't wait for this to be finished and took bets with the boys as to what kind of ship it would be. Perhaps a pirate ship displaying the skull and crossbones flag? A yacht? A luxury liner? How disappointed we were when we saw the finished object — a long, grey concrete structure, with what was supposed to be a funnel at one end and a slightly raised square just beneath. We had wonderful imaginations, however, and created all kinds of weird and wonderful games from the "bow" of our ship.

Sometimes we made the younger children line up at the edge of the pool, encouraging them to throw leaves and branches at us. We then retaliated by splashing them with as much water as our shoes would hold, they being the only receptacles to hand. Despite the hours we spent in the water none of us ever learned to swim there, perhaps because the water came up to our knees, even in its deepest section.

On warm, summer afternoons, standing on the raised section of our ship, I pretended I was Cleopatra sailing down the Nile, eager to see my beloved Anthony. If it rained I imagined I was shipwrecked and had been washed up on some exotic shore where my true love would be waiting for me. The other children shouted and screamed as they played out their own fantasies, but I was immune to their cries.

We loved it best of all when it rained, for then we all pretended we were in a submarine, on the look-out for the enemy. As the skies darkened and the rain lashed down, our Jim shouted, at the top of his voice and in his best "British" accent, "Up periscope", or "Dive, dive!", being an avid follower of all the war films that were shown in those days. Lying flat on the cold, wet surface, eyes searching for our adversaries, hearts pounding with excitement, we "killed" the enemy, passers-by who were totally unaware of our game, by calling out "That one's mine", pointing with our fingers to where the unsuspecting person was. We were always the victors, maybe because most of the other children had gone home the minute it started to rain!

The tennis courts, enclosed behind high wire-mesh fencing, attracted all of us, adults and children alike. On warm, lazy summer days we lined up outside the perimeter, our heads bobbing left and right as the would-be tennis "stars", brilliant white shorts atop well-muscled legs, airtex shirts gleaming blue-white in the sun, showed off their prowess. After the game we watched with envy as they enjoyed a picnic of strawberries, cream, small sandwiches and always, a huge bottle of lemonade. Finally replete they lounged against the wire mesh, sucking big Jaffa oranges, the tangy scent of the freshly-peeled fruit hovering in the warm air, causing my taste buds to itch with longing.

None of us could afford to play tennis there, even if

we could have afforded the fees we didn't have the right attire. I loved the sound of the ball as it hit the racket and often wished I could join in. When I eventually did have a game, many years later and on an indoor court, I didn't enjoy it at all. My Mother always said that wanting something and having it were often two entirely different things, and she was right.

Quite often, after Sunday Mass, we all trooped into the park, after first spending our collection pennies on "illicit" ice-lollies at the local sweet shop. The smell of orangeade, lime juice and raspberry juice more than made up for guilt at having deprived God of those few pennies. I have made my peace with Him since those days and feel sure he wouldn't have begrudged us our bit of pleasure. Sweets were a luxury then, only enjoyed once a week, not even that if the breadwinner was out of work.

In a roundabout way I suppose I was punished for my sin as, one Sunday I was racing home from Mass (and after just catching the tail-end of Father O'Keefe's sermon) down Wright Street when suddenly I was knocked flat. Closing my eyes in embarrassment I suddenly smelled something fetid close to my face and felt a sharp pin-type prick on my hand. On opening my eyes I was confronted by the dribbling jaw of a dog, who had obviously ran out of an entry just as I was passing. In panic I jumped to my feet, pushing the dog out of the way, and turned to grab my little sister's hand, dropping my arm with a gasp of pain.

Mother said God moves in mysterious ways and she was right, for I had broken my arm and it was many

138

Sundays before I was able to enjoy the pleasures of the park.

Sometimes we gathered on the covered bandstand, if it wasn't being used by one of the few remaining bands or the Salvation Army, and play cowboys and Indians, the girls playing squaws because the boys wouldn't allow us to be anything else. Sometimes I was Scarlett O'Hara, (although my "Southern Belle" accent sounded very strange due to my "Brummie" background!), having not long before read Margaret Mitchell's *Gone with the Wind*, waiting on the "terrace" for handsome Rhett Butler to come and claim me! Part of me admired her independence, yet the softer side of me abhorred her treatment of the gorgeous Rhett! The other girls laughed at me but I didn't care so lost was I in fantasy!

There used to be a drinking fountain half-way along the main pathway into the park and, one day, I was pushed forward as I bent to take a drink, and still bear the legacy — a slight chip in one of my front teeth! The water tasted wonderful and was far more refreshing than our tap water at home, especially after we'd been playing hop-scotch or "tag" for hours on end. While the boys played cricket or football, the latter strongly forbidden by the park-keeper, we girls sat on the grass making daisy chains and trying to make a blade of sweet-smelling grass whistle. In our early teenage years we played "He loves me, he loves me not" by pulling the petals off the daises, one by one, and throwing them on the grass, much to the dismay of the park-keeper. I don't know why we did it because, at that stage in our lives, we didn't know who "he" was!

I loved the names of the streets in that area — Wordsworth, Byron, Tennyson etc. When the daffodils were in full bloom, such a contrast to our blue-brick cobbled yard, their bright yellow heads lifted to the sun, all at identical height, I softly recited Wordsworth's famous poem as I savoured the smell and sight of those innocent flowers. Their fragrance waited around me as I carried home a small bouquet, purchased from Wheeler's for just a few pennies, for my Mother's solitary flower vase. The pleasure they gave her lasted long after they'd lost their scent.

I had to take not only my own three sisters to Mass and the park, but also some of the neighbours' children. It was murder! How I never lost any of them I'll never know. One afternoon I pushed my youngest sister Jean, then just six months old, into a laurel bush so the rest of us could play in peace. We were half-way home before our Jim realised we'd left her behind! Hearts pounding, it was now nearly dusk, we raced back to find her peacefully sleeping, just as we had left her. After picking off the few leaves that had stuck to her hair, and removing some tiny insects from her clothing, she was none the worse for her experience. To this day my Mother is unaware of the incident. At the time she did comment on the strange, musty smell which seemed to seep from Jean's clothing when she undressed her!

Guy Fawkes Night in the park was wonderful! Enormous bonfires, strictly controlled, fantastic fireworks displays, hot potatoes for sale, chestnuts, too hot to handle, the sights, smells and sounds were indescribable. The bonfires, fuelled by all manner of things, were so high I could never see the top. The carnival-like atmosphere lived long in the memories of us all. I loved the smoky smell of the different kinds of wood, but Mum didn't like having to try and cleanse it from our clothes.

On hot summer days Mother accompanied us to the park, the baby's pram loaded with all the things she thought were necessary for a day out. Bits of sheeting, "to dry yourselves with after a dip in the pool", thick wedges of bread and jam, the pungent aroma of the black currants tickling our taste buds on the journey there; her straw hat "to keep off the sun", "vanishing" cream — "in case you get burnt" and milk bottles filled with home-made lemonade, made by mixing kaylie (a sort of lemon flavoured powdery substance) with cold water — delicious. We once used rainbow-coloured kaylie but it didn't taste the same at all.

These outings with Mother were more restricted as we had to stay within her sight at all times, but we didn't really mind for we knew, if we behaved ourselves all the next week we could back there — alone!

Before going home we rubbed out our chalked hop-scotch pitch and replaced the bits of grass the boys had dug up for their cricket games. Pleasantly tired we strolled slowly home, each of us wrapped up in our own pleasures of the day.

Such fun we had — and all for free!

CHAPTER
FIFTEEN

Wet, Wet, Wet!

Cold,
wet,
smelly,
water.

River,
stream,
pool,
water.

Green,
blue,
grey,
water.

All
wanting
to devour
ME!

Water, Water.

I hate water, especially in the swimming baths at Green Lane. All the other girls used to love going there, but not me. Even walking down Little Green Lane towards the baths was torture, the ozone-laden air caused me to sneeze and cough before I entered the huge, cavernous bathing area of the baths. The water had a cloying, pungent smell which I am sure didn't do my weak chest any good, although my doctor decreed otherwise!

I tried every ploy I knew to get out of swimming lessons, but to no avail, mainly due to the doctor telling my Mother that the exercise would be very good for me. He may well have been right regarding my physical health but it certainly didn't do my nerves any good.

The first time I went, at the age of eleven, I stood shaking on the side of the baths, holding my breath in an effort not to inhale the dreadful odour. All the other girls were splashing about, enjoying every moment, and I thought they were mad. The teacher urged me to join my fellow classmates, which took up nearly half of my first lesson! When I finally plucked up the courage to climb down the metal ladder, hanging on for dear life, my heart was thumping painfully. Encouraged by the teacher I inched slowly downwards, dreading the moment when my feet hit the water. When they did it was every bit as bad as I'd feared. It was so different to splashing about in a few inches of water in the paddling pool at the park. Leaving me to adjust myself, the teacher started the lesson. The other girls glowered at me as I stood, shivering from head to foot, by the handrail around the baths. I could taste salt on my lips and wasn't surprised, on wiping them, to find droplets of blood on my fingers. No-one seemed to understand my fear and I hated the teacher for laughing and telling the other girls I was a "baby".

The other girls were all lying on their backs in a circle, holding hands with the girl next to them. Nothing would induce me to join that circle. Miserably I hugged the rail harder and tried to will myself to be anywhere but there. "Please, God" I prayed, "just get me out of here — I promise I'll do anything you want if you'll only let me go!" Needless to say He didn't hear me, but the teacher did.

Gripping my arm, she hissed "Now, come on, Mary, don't be silly, nothing will happen to you. Besides" she added "you're holding up the lesson!" None too gently she prised my fingers off the rail and steered me towards the other girls. My legs were shaking and I was on the verge of tears. Chiding me for being silly, she urged me into the huge circle, saying "Just hold hands with Diane and Ann, then lift up your feet — the water will support you". Slowly I attempted to do as she asked and ended up, flat on my back, on the slippery bottom of the pool, inhaling large lungfuls of obnoxious tasting water in the process. My lesson, for that day anyway, was over.

I think part of my fear stemmed from a couple of bad experiences I had when very young. Aunt Cissie, my mother's eldest sister (and also my Godmother), arrived on a visit from her home in London. It was a beautiful summer day and she took me into Birmingham to buy me a new dress. I remember being excited as I hadn't been into the city centre before, only passed through on the way to my regular visits to the Children's Hospital. Gripping me tightly by the hand she outlined her plans for the day, first we'd shop, then we'd go to one of the big shops to have something to eat and drink.

She bought me a beautiful pale lemon dress and lemon ribbons to match, for my hair. We went up in the lift of Lewis's, and each time it stopped to allow others to enter, the exciting, enticing smells invaded the small, square room. Perfumes, new clothes, beautiful fabrics, their varying scents filling my head to such an extent that I was over-excited before we reached the roof. I remember how pleased I felt when I saw all the chairs and tables set out on the roof, and being able to see for miles over the city. In the centre was a small paddling pool and lots of children were splashing about, laughing and shouting. Cautioning me to stay away from the pool while she ordered our food, Aunt Cissie wandered off to secure a table.

The sun was dancing on the sparkling blue-green water and, mesmerised, I moved ever closer. So enthralled was I by the diamond-shaped, glittering lights on the surface I failed to hear a warning shout.

The next thing I remember was the journey home on the bus, wrapped in Aunt Cissie's fur coat (she always wore that fur coat, whatever the weather), all my clothing a soggy mass in the bottom of her shopping bag. The whole episode stayed in my mind, highlighted every time I smelled coffee, due to the fact that someone on the roof that day was drinking the dark, bitter liquid. That dreadful experience, unfortunately, marred my pleasure in our outings to Lewis's as we grew older.

A few months after my return from the convalescent home Mrs H asked if she could take me to the seaside for the day, assuring my Mother it would do me good. Denis and Jim were really envious and Jim teased me about sea monsters and other such awful creatures. I knew he was lying because my Father had told me all about the sea, having been brought up very close to it at home in Ireland. I couldn't wait to see the boats, the fishermen, the seagulls and the little fishes and didn't sleep at all the night before the promised trip.

We travelled by train from Snow Hill Station, and I loved the smoky, steamy atmosphere and the smell of hissing coals as the engine huffed and puffed before the start of its journey. The roof of the station was made of glass, so high I hurt my neck staring up at it. White smoke billowed up into the air and I remember taking deep breaths of it, its moist, tarry smell oozing up into my nostrils and down into my chest. I didn't realise I had turned purple until Mr H pulled me away from it!

I trembled with excitement, as did most of the other children there that day, their buckets and spades swinging from their hands. Mrs H said she would buy me a bucket and spade when we got to the seaside. We passed through many small towns that day, but my favourite was when we got out into the country. The smells invaded the train and some of the adults actually closed their windows. I was surprised, for to me the smells were fresh, clean, new and I revelled in them. I waved to cows, sheep and horses and even farmers, in fact anyone who looked up at the train! My excitement must have been catching for quite a few of the passengers smiled at Mr and Mrs H and said "Is it her first time on a train?".

I will never forget my first sight of the sea — it was enormous. A slight breeze wafted over me bringing exciting smells I had never known before. The salty tang of cockles and mussels, fish and chips and the sea itself lives on in my memory. Sticky, fluffy candy floss, toffee apples, their taste hitherto unknown, were mine for the asking. Dragging my eyes away from the side stalls I gazed, awe-struck at the ocean. My first thought was, it isn't blue like in my picture books. Where were the little sea horses, the tiny fishes, the boats?

Mrs H took my hand and whispered "Would you like to have a little paddle, love?". Nervously I nodded, and she took off my new white socks and black patent leather shoes. I recoiled as the cold, wet, blue-grey water covered my feet, and ran screaming along the wet, sandy beach. A piece of seaweed wrapped itself around one foot and I screamed even louder. I thought a sea-monster had risen from its bed to eat me.

Mr H chased after me and I turned my head, then bumped into something warm and smelly. With horror I looked round, I was standing next to a donkey — its yellow teeth bared and I screamed again. Nothing Mr and Mrs H could do would pacify me — I wanted to go home immediately. Looking back I feel so sorry that I caused that lovely couple so much grief. Their own daughter had, sadly, died at the age of five and I don't think they ever recovered from her death. Mother often

147

said that, in me, Mrs H saw reflections of her own little girl, which was why she was so fond of me.

Those two experiences put me off water for life!

The paddling pools in the park never held any fears for me. I was too busy splashing about, playing our games of make-believe to worry about danger. Sometimes I would pretend I was a mermaid and would lie, face down (but with my head held well above water level), moving my arms in a swimming motion. My body always stayed in exactly the same position because my knees were resting on the bottom of the pool.

I tried everything I knew to save myself the horrors of the school swimming lessons, forging Mother's signature on notes which said I had anything from Verrucas to a "bad" stomach. Sometimes the teacher believed them and sometimes she didn't. One day I did actually manage to lie in the circle, flat on my back — which wasn't as bad as I'd feared. I even kidded myself I was enjoying it. That all changed when we were told "flip over on your tummies, girls". That was my undoing and I have never forgotten the bleach-type taste of the water I swallowed that day.

Eventually the teacher decided I would never learn to swim, so I was given extra English to do instead, which wasn't a hardship.

My younger sister, Theresa, dearly wanted to learn to swim and so, greatly daring, I accompanied her one summer evening to the baths. We stood at the side for ages, watching the children splashing about. Suddenly Theresa disappeared from my side and landed, with a loud splash, in the water. Frantically I looked around for help, shouting "Hang on, bab, I'll get someone — don't panic". It was just as well she didn't panic for, by the time I found a lifeguard, she would have drowned. Instead, she struck out blindly and when I returned with the lifeguard, she was grinning like a Cheshire Cat, shouting "Look at me, Mary, I can swim!". She certainly was and, for one brief moment, I wished it had been me who had been accidentally pushed in. Although, on reflection, I would probably have drowned.

Whenever I use bleach these days I am back in the nightmare world of Green Lane Swimming Baths. Even today I can't swim, being a firm believer that if God had wanted me to he would have given me fins instead of arms. I can't say my enjoyment on family holidays has suffered because of it, except when I watch my husband, who is a very strong swimmer, plough through the water like a shark, leaving me at the edge to paddle with the toddlers! I now love the sea, in all its moods, but am quite happy not to envelop myself in its depths!

The "cut" (or canal as the grown-ups referred to it), in Garrison Lane, had a strange, spicy type of smell emanating from its green, litter-strewn water. Tall weed lined both banks, resting lazily against the rusty, corrugated sheeting placed there by the factory owners. Occasionally a brightly-coloured barge, carrying coal, steel or some other commodity, would appear and I would dream about the exotic, far-off places the goods came from, and whence they were going.

In my daydreams the water meandered to the sea, to be welcomed by warm, lapping waves. In reality it ran under a hump-backed bridge at one end of the lane and, sluggishly, made its heavy way to its destination. In winter the spicy smell diminished to be replaced with a subtle, tangy tantalising aroma. Whether it came from the bits of coal or whatever falling off the barges, or the plant life living far below its murky depths, I don't know. I inhaled great gulps of it in the hope that it would clear my bad chest!

I told my sisters many stories about the cut, of mythical creatures that lived in its depths, who all had wonderful names. Theresa the Terrapin was kind and caring, Jean the jelly-fish was a small, warm creature, and Chris the crocodile was the queen of the cut, but kind to her fellow creatures. My sisters loved them all, especially the fact that I used their names for the characters in my stories.

I have crossed the sea a few times since then and messed about in boats on many various ponds and rivers, but none of them ever had the same, secret smell in their depths. On one boating trip, quite a few years ago now, a huge water rat almost jumped into our boat, causing my heart to leap with fear — not of the rat but of the gallons of water waiting to devour me.

Water is definitely not my most favourite thing!

CHAPTER
SIXTEEN

Sun, Sea and Sand?

Ice cream,
candy floss,
circus fun —
no sun.

Sightseeing,
train ride,
being free —
no sea.

Busy traffic,
noise, fumes,
hardcore land —
no sand.

Holidays

We didn't have "real" holidays, such as at the seaside, but we were lucky in that my Mother's family had moved to London after the Second World War and we visited them nearly every summer of my childhood.

The holiday started with the ride on the train, which I loved. The hissing and spitting of the engine, the smoky atmosphere fills my head even today. On arrival at Euston Station, a huge, exciting place invaded by all kinds of smells, not all of them pleasant, we would all take deep breaths then quickly scan the crowds for our first sight of Aunt Cissie, Mother's eldest sister. Her hugs and kisses, and the tears when she first espied us, were well worth waiting a whole year for. Aunt Cissie had been widowed, at the age of just thirty-eight, and left to bring up five small children alone, the youngest being only two at the time. She was, and still is, amazing and I always wanted to be just like her.

Her round, bespectacled face, was always glowing with health and laughter, topped by a mop of curly black hair, which was always awry as if she was constantly running her fingers through it. Her matronly figure, enwrapped in either a smart grey or blue two-piece suit, its straight skirt straining at the seams, or a pretty floral dress covered with a long white cardigan, would bustle towards us and she and my Mother would cry copious tears of happiness on each other's shoulders.

Sometimes we would board the bus to take us to her home in Streatham but, if it was raining she would hail one of the many passing taxis, a treat indeed for us. I much preferred the top deck of the big red bus, from there I could see all the exciting people and places the capital offered. My first sight of the Thames made me feel restless somehow, and I couldn't wait to walk along its banks with my cousins during the coming weeks. The Houses of Parliament, so beautiful in the summer sunshine, twinkled happily as we passed by, its exterior belying the seriousness of its hallowed halls. The unexpected smell of fish and chips would float along the length of the bus, causing my tummy to rumble and my mouth to water, and I forgot about everything except arriving at the flat and enjoying one of Aunt Cissie's "gourmet delights".

She was a wonderful, if haphazard cook, conjuring up delicious, if strange concoctions for us to enjoy. Very rarely did she cook the kind of meals we had at home, being a firm believer in "meat and two veg". I remember the first time she gave us butter beans (ugh) and being upset because I thought she meant green beans with butter spread on them! Meals were taken when we felt hungry, which in itself was unusual as we had set times at home. To keep us going during our hours of play she or Gran would make up big, thick sandwiches of ham, or boiled egg for us to take out, which we devoured almost immediately.

The flat contained three bedrooms, a large square living room and a small kitchen, plus bathroom and toilet. The bliss of not having to go out in the dark to the toilet, and of being able to take a bath inside a proper bathroom instead of the old tin bath by the fire, was all part and parcel of the joys of that particular holiday. The furniture was well-worn, but always clean and shining, due to the efforts of both Gran and Aunt Cissie, the former never seen without either a duster or teatowel tucked into the belt of her apron. All this, coupled with the wonders of electricity, television, and a proper radiogram was luxury indeed.

The flat was filled to bursting point, for not only did Gran and Grandad live with Aunt Cissie, but all five of her children! We shared beds with our cousins, sleeping "top to tail", and talking and giggling long into the night, catching up on all the family news, until Grandad thumped on the adjoining wall with his walking stick!

Grandad was very tall, in complete contrast to Gran who was about five feet nothing and as broad as she was tall. He wore his silvery hair brushed back off his forehead, adding even mare length to his long, thin face. His dark navy-blue pin-striped suit, pressed to within an inch of its life by Gran, covered a white, collarless shirt, open at the neck where small silver hairs poked through, and black leather, highly-polished shoes on his size eleven feet! I never saw him dressed in casual clothes, but don't think they would have suited him anyway.

I loved the smell of the pipe Grandad smoked and if I catch a hint of Erinmore tobacco today I am back in Aunt Cissie's crowded living room, sitting close to Grandad as he bent over the Sporting Life paper, working out his doubles and trebles for that day. He was crazy about the horses, Mother said it was because he'd spent his life driving a dray and used to groom the horses and enter them for shows, taking a well-deserved pat on the back from the owners when they won a rosette. I just

154

thought he liked to gamble! Sometimes he would hiss "Oh, Jasus!", and closing his eyes would stab blindly with his pencil at the runners, murmuring "Oh, sure he's no chance at all, at all!", and go on studying form. When he did have a little win he would always slip us children a few coppers "for your sweeties".

Mother's other sister, Teenie, lived with her husband and family in the same block as Aunt Cissie, a couple of floors up. Walking into her living room was like stepping into another world. Beautiful, highly-polished furniture adorned the lounge, the three-piece moquette suite in shades of blue taking pride of place, its pristine covers still retaining their new smell. The kitchen had all the latest gadgets of the day and I loved to watch Aunt Teenie at work in there. She was a very pretty, blonde lady, who loved make-up, jewellery and perfumes. She wore Chanel No. 5 and Blue Grass and always gave me the empty containers, which I cherished, sniffing at the stopper even when there was nothing left to smell!

Uncle Eddie, Teenie's husband, ran a wet fish stall at Covent Garden and, no matter how often he bathed, never seemed to lose the pungent smell. He played the accordion, the squeeze box and anything else he could coax a tune from, and we spent many happy hours listening to him and joining in with songs of the "owld days", all three families crammed into the lounge, the place ringing with sound. Happy days indeed.

We spent many happy hours wandering the streets of London and it seemed the sun always shone then. We visited St. James Palace, watched the Changing of the Guard, their handsome faces stern under the bearskins. I always felt sorry for them as the heat must have been unbearable at times, yet I never saw any of them sweating! We couldn't afford to visit the Tower of London or Madame Tussauds, or indeed any place which cost more than a few pennies to enter, but were more than content with what we did manage to see.

Battersea Fun Fair was a constant source of delight to us all, and with the few pennies Gran slipped to us, unaware that Grandad had also given us threepence each if he'd had a bit of luck on the horses, we'd exhaust the thrills the fair had on offer, returning home tired, hungry but ecstatic. The smells from that fair remain with me today, hot-dogs, ice-cream, candy-floss, manure (the latter via the animals) and human excitement. Whilst our skin gently tanned, without the aid of sun factors and creams, our minds would slowly relax as we revelled in the space and freedom of London.

The Odeon Cinema on the Streatham "High Road" was a rare treat but sometimes Gran would beg us to take her. The inside of this grand place was far more luxurious than our own cinemas. Huge burgundy curtains covered the screen, the velvet swaying gently in the breeze from vents in the ceiling. The seats seemed deeper and more comfortable somehow, their velvety fabric seeped in long-ago smells, camphor, ice-cream and, now and then, a hint of fish! On one occasion Gran begged us to take her to see *Sleeping Beauty*, then snored all the way through the film! On waking, her bright blue eyes twinkling, double chins wobbling, she said, voice husky with sleep, "Sure wasn't that a lovely filum"! We all loved her dearly.

Streatham Common was our playground, its vastness a welcome change from the confines of the yard. Here we played all kinds of hitherto unknown games, devised by our cousins. As well as the usual hide and seek, rounders and tag, we became soldiers as we fought medieval battles, dive-bombers in the Second World War, duellists during the French Revolution, all the while hugging the knowledge that the kids in Small Heath were unaware of such games. We couldn't wait to get back to the yard to show off.

A couple of my female cousins took me to the West End one day and I was over-awed by its theatres, the glitter of the wonderful shops, the enticing exciting smells, but was terrified of the traffic. On another occasion we walked, open-mouthed, through Soho, staring at photographs of scantily-clad girls displayed outside sleazy-looking establishments, girls, partially-clothed, lounging in dark doorways and tramps lying under newspapers and cardboard boxes. I had never seen anything like it in Brum, and found it hard to relate the scenes I beheld with the affluence of the London portrayed in the press.

To my surprise Petticoat Lane wasn't the long, meandering lane I'd envisaged, but a hotch-potch of stall-laden side-streets, filled with noise, colour and smells. Every smell was new and exciting; oriental spices, pease-pudding, new bread, leather, curry and human sweat. I purchased a string of blue beads from one of the stall-holders with the shiny sixpence Grandad had slipped into my hand the previous evening, their smooth oblong shape soothing to the touch. As I slipped them over my head a strange, orangey smell drifted into my nostrils, giving me a tantalising glimpse of some far-off, wonderful land. No matter how many times I washed those beads the smell remained.

Theresa and I were chosen as bridesmaids for our cousin Margaret's wedding, at a big church in the heart of London. It was the first time since my First Communion I had the opportunity to wear a "posh" frock. Mine was knee length, pale lemon chiffon with a frilled hem, short puffed sleeves and a huge bow tied at the back. Around my head I wore a coronet of real roses, their scent so enjoyable to me but, also, unfortunately to the wasps! My cousin cast me baleful looks as I dodged this way and that during the photo session, in my attempts to get away from the horrible insects! Theresa looked gorgeous in her dress, her long black hair teased into ringlets especially for the occasion, her pretty face serene, even when the wasps attacked her head-dress. She was three years younger then me and I envied her that wonderful poise which she possessed from a very young age.

I don't remember much of the ceremony but do recall the fantastic hotel in which the wedding breakfast was held. I expected to eat bacon and eggs and was very surprised to find that it wasn't that kind of breakfast! Huge sparkling crystal chandeliers adorned the ornate ceilings, glistening glasses tinkled as the toast was made, and real china plates, edged in gold, held our food. Picking up the heavy silver cutlery I turned it over and over in my hands, marvelling at the smoothness and elegance of a piece of metal! I was amazed at the number of plates and dishes used for that meal for, at home, if we were having a desert we washed up the dinner plates and re-used them!

The scent of roses, from my cousin's bouquet, the table decorations, our posies and head-dresses, mingled with the savoury aroma of roast beef, their differing scents lingering long in my memory. Dancing afterwards to a three-piece band, the men in black tail-coats, looking rather like penguins to me, were all elderly but played music such as I had never heard before, Strauss, Mozart and others of their ilk. Every time I hear *The Blue Danube* I see again that glittering occasion, and can smell the rose-scented air. For me it was one of the most exciting days of my life so far, especially when my cousin Robert (who was then fourteen) said he would like to marry me one day! My Mother overheard him, blessed herself and cried "No, never, first cousins can't marry child, so get it out of your heads!", taking some of the shine from that day. When I asked Father O'Keefe about it some weeks later he shook his shaggy head and said, mournfully, "Oh Mary, my dear child, you're far too young to think of marriage! Besides", he added "when the time does come you must promise me, and your God, that you won't marry your first cousin!". Crossing my heart I gave my promise and was so pleased that Robert married someone else many years later!

I met some Pearly Kings and Queens on one occasion and watched in amazement as everyone around them started dancing The Lambeth Walk, my feet itching to

159

join in but my soul too shy. The colours, the sounds and the smells remain with me to this day.

All too soon the holiday was at end, amid tears and laughter we boarded the train, our hearts forlorn. As soon as the train came to rest in Snow Hill Station we were rejuvenated, thinking of all the stories we had to tell to our friends, the memories we would carry forever in our hearts and, smiling, would board the bus for home. Who needed the boring old seaside anyway!

CHAPTER
SEVENTEEN

How Much?

She came in every Saturday
for a pair of stockings "lisle",
that little old lady
with the Mona Lisa smile.

She proffered her one shilling,
watching me all the while,
sweet old lady
with the Mona Lisa smile.

"They're one and six" I'd mutter,
as my colleague, in the aisle,
stared at the old lady
with the Mona Lisa smile.

Shaking her greying head
she'd turn, and think awhile,
cute old lady
with the Mona Lisa smile.

"I'm only a pensioner"
she'd say, with artless guile,

lovely old lady
with the Mona Lisa smile.

She cost me a fortune,
with her wit and wile,
canny old lady
with the Mona Lisa smile!

Work

When I was about fourteen years old Father asked if I was willing to do some typing for his boss on Saturdays. I was thrilled, for not only would it give me the edge on my class-mates in the typing class, but meant I would be relieved of my usual Saturday chores. The fact that I would receive the princely sum of ten shillings (fifty new pence) for my labours was immaterial — at first anyway.

At that time Father worked for a scrap-car dealer in Aston, and often regaled me with tales of the people who worked there, and the various characters who bought the old bangers. I couldn't wait to start my temporary employment, mainly so I could brag to my friends at school that I was working! (Father O'Keefe did have a word in my ear the following week about being big-headed, but smiled when he said it, so I think he was only joking!)

To say I was disappointed is an under-statement, instead of rows and rows of slightly damaged cars as I'd envisaged, bits and pieces of them were piled, haphazardly, in a huge, greasy yard. The once-gleaming paint work scratched and scarred, the powerful engines silenced forever. Tyres of varying sizes were piled higgeldy-piggeldy in one large corner of the yard, some with inner tubes hanging out, looking to me like deflated balloons. To me it seemed a graveyard, for that is what it resembled, minus the headstones. Squat A40s jostled for space with Hillman Minxes, and a once glorious, silver bonnet (I think it belonged to a Zephyr) peeped

163

out furtively from the side of the mound, its tyre-less wheels obscenely naked.

I felt sad as I envisaged the miles all those vehicles had travelled, the wonderful places they must have seen, carrying proud owners to their destinations, only to end up in this cheerless place, which reeked of rubber, oil and decay.

The customers seemed to enjoy scrambling over the unevenly stacked cars in their search for alternators, distributors and whatever. Some of them climbed on top of the piles of tyres, oblivious to the dust and grease staining their clothes. They reminded me of my brothers and their friends playing on the bombed sites!

The office was also in a sorry state, files piled on every available, dusty surface. Mr J, tall, slightly bald, protruding stomach, fat cigar clenched in his fist, assured me they'd only been that way since his secretary had taken ill. His twinkling eyes smiled all the time, and as the first day wore on I understood why my Father enjoyed working there.

All the men were friendly, calling me their "tempting" secretary, which brought a blush to my face and joy to my heart. Bernie, the break-down truck driver, was the epitome of what I believed truck-drivers should be. His sandy hair, slightly receding at the temples, still held a few curls which he was always slicking down with handfuls of water. He wore a sleeveless jerkin, made of some kind of shiny dark blue material, over his check shirt, the sleeves of which were always rolled up to his elbows. On top of this he wore a donkey jacket, making his huge shoulders look even bigger. His hands were huge, covered in freckles, short, thick nails ragged at the edges. His voice was beautiful, deep as a baritone, and he once told me he had sung in a choir at home in Wales. I loved to listen to him sing in Welsh, which he did at the top of his voice, when working in the yard. Sometimes the other men would join in, singing in English, creating unlikely harmonies!

The name of Bernie's after-shave, was unknown to me, smelling of the sea on a winter's day, and I adored it. When he stood near me I inhaled deeply of the aroma, closing my eyes in ecstasy. Heaven knows what he thought!

I thoroughly enjoyed the six Saturdays I spent in "my" office, a tiny, warm room, its-once-upon-a-time sunshine yellow walls now mellowed to a kind of tobacco colour, due to the constant smoking of Mr J and all his men. Everything smelled of engine oil, grease, correcting fluid (I wasn't a very proficient typist at that time!), tobacco, and good, strong Typhoo tea.

To some people the smell would have been obnoxious, but to me it was wonderful. Even today when I catch a hint of oil, or use Typhoo tea, it takes me back to that time, and the warm, smiling faces of Mr J, my Father and the other men as I battled with the old Imperial, "sit up and beg" typewriter, the mucky carbon paper, and the ribbon that always seemed to run out at a vital point in my work!

One of the highlights of my few weeks there was the ride home on the break-down truck. Squashed between the tweed jacket of my Father, and the thick padded donkey jacket of Bernie, I felt like a Queen surveying my domain from the high seat of the cab. Another highlight was the bag of freshly cooked chips Father bought me, soaked in salt and vinegar, then washed down with a good cup of tea. As we ate, the men squatting on whatever surface was available, their faces wreathed in smiles, they teased me unmercifully about boyfriends, causing me to blush. Their good natured bantering gave me a very good grounding for my real working life, and I think it is because of those lovely men that I finally outgrew my shyness.

My second foray into the working world was as a Saturday Girl at Woolworth's on the Coventry Road, when I was fifteen. Quite a few of the girls from the fifth year at school applied for jobs there, most being taken on. We had to take a maths test prior to the interview, and I failed mine — twice! Luckily enough the Supervisor kindly gave me a third, and final, chance, and to my surprise I passed! I must be honest though, if it hadn't been for the fact that Katy, one of the girls from my year, was also taking her test at the same time, I wouldn't have passed. Thanks, Katy. I did confess to Father O'Keefe, who was sadly disappointed in me, but then said "If you'd have had more time to think about the answers, do you think you would have passed easily?", and I was very pleased to confirm that I would.

Wonderful Woolies was a dream! Its hard wooden floor, swept daily and polished with a huge buffer, smelled delicious. Other smells filled the air, from the spicy scent of ginger biscuits, angel cake, mint imperials, Palmolive and Knights Castile soaps, Amami setting lotion, to the more mundane smells of firewood and plastic pac-a-macs, creating an Aladdin's Cave of aromas! I was a little put out to be installed on the Haberdashery counter, away from most of the enticing scents.

My overall was so large I had to put elastic bands around my elbows to prevent the sleeves from continually failing over my hands, and my arms bore the red weals for a long time. I didn't care at all, for I was only too happy to be working there at all.

On entering through the huge, glass doors each Saturday morning, at around eight thirty, I felt as if I was entering a different World. The hushed atmosphere, at that time of the day, was not dissimilar to that of my Church, although the smells were entirely different. Climbing the old, wooden stairs to the staff room, the enticing smell of hot buttered toast wafting down from the "canteen", I wanted to dance a jig of sheer happiness, but refrained lest the supervisor think I was mad! One by the one the other girls arrived, chatting and laughing, and the room filled with noise. Precisely at eight forty-five, the Floor Supervisor, fob watch pinned to her smart uniform, appeared to check our appearance before sending us down to the shop floor.

My heart leaped with excitement every time I stepped behind the high, wooden counter, impatient for the customers to arrive. There were four counters around the haberdashery stall, forming an oblong shape. Inside these two tills reposed, one at either side of the long display shelves. I enjoyed selling my goods, and especially loved the feel of the "just like silk" ties and scarves, their "new" smell remaining on my fingers long after.

Real nylon stockings lay in serried rows, their crinkly plastic wrappers a delight to the touch. Bras, from size 28A cup (which was too big for me unfortunately!), lay, naked, alongside knickers and vests, in neat piles down the length of the counter. Lisle stockings, thick and heavy, were placed discreetly beneath the more luxurious items. Ribbons, beads, and knitting wools, their glorious colours shining in the mellow lighting, were either coiled around pieces of card or draped from hooks on stainless steel rods. Cards of buttons and safety pins fitted neatly into small niches built into the counter. Men's woollen socks nestled against the latest, brightly coloured "bobby" socks, their black, brown and dark blue shades high-lighting even more the psychedelic colours of the new fashion craze!

Paper dress patterns, their plain white covers hiding the secrets of the popular shift dresses, flared skirts and crisp, cotton blouses, jostled for space with the knitting and crochet patterns. I longed then for the knowledge I had so blithely ignored during sewing lessons. Fingering the glossy printed pages I prayed for the skill to turn the pictures into wonderful jumpers, cardigans and tam-o'-shanters a few balls of wool could create.

When the Blues were playing a home game the atmosphere inside the store was electric. The Manager and his staff walked slowly down the gangways between the counters, eyes darting to every blue and white scarf, on the lookout for trouble and petty theft. The boys in blue always approached my counter, especially if my

Supervisor wasn't around, to taunt me, picking up bras, slyly asking which size I took! Somehow I handled their comments, trying to still the trembling in my hands as I retrieved the articles from their grasp. By the time they'd left my counter resembled a jumble sale, which I hastily put to rights before my Supervisor's return. I don't ever remember there being any trouble with any of the football fans then, either inside our store or out in the streets.

Every other Saturday a very poor-looking, elderly lady, smelling strongly of onions, hovered at my stall, her long, gnarled fingers tentatively picking up a pair of lisle stockings. No matter how often I told her they cost one shilling and sixpence (under eight pence), she only ever proffered one shilling, (five new pence), pretending she was deaf when I requested the extra money! Mumbling so I had to strain to hear, the querulous voice hissed "I'm only a pensioner, dear!", then almost slyly "Do you have a Granny, dear", immediately making me visualise my own, lovely Gran not being able to afford something so mundane as a a pair of lisle stockings! That image was my undoing, and I made the mistake of letting her have one pair for just one shilling, then paid the penalty throughout the rest of my working days there. Every Saturday, when the Supervisor was making up the tills, I advised her that I owed it sixpence, explaining why. Wryly she remarked that the "dear" old lady had been pulling that trick for as long as she could remember!

Having to hand over sixpence out of my pay of sixteen shillings and fourpence (less than eighty new pence), seemed a small price to pay for a little old lady's pleasure. When I told Father O'Keefe, instead of the praise I'd expected from him, he told me it was wrong to boast about helping people less fortunate than ourselves. A lesson I have never forgotten.

At five-thirty, after placing the takings, carefully checked by my Supervisor, into small, cloth bags before taking them upstairs to the safe, we covered our counters with huge calico sheets, smelling faintly of dust and mothballs. Our wages were paid out in the canteen, and I was thrilled that, at last, I could purchase a pair of proper nylons, out of my own money! It was a great feeling. Once downstairs again, the cleaners already busy with brooms and polish, we were ushered into the street, and I always felt bereft as I cast a long, lingering look at "my" counter, feeling happy that in just a few days I would be ensconced there once more.

My first "real" job was as Junior Secretary to the Accounts Manager at a huge, holloware factory in Hockley. On my very first day (16 July 1962) I arrived, breathless after running all the way from the bus-stop, green school mac flapping around my thighs as Mother said I wasn't to go out without it being as it was raining quite heavily. When I reached the top of the stairs I bumped into the imposing figure of the Company Secretary. He, on seeing my small, bedraggled figure, asked where was my Mother, and I recall the look of surprise on his face when I told him who I was and who I would be working for. Wordlessly he motioned me to follow him, down miles of endless corridors, eventually stopping in front of a door, identical to all the other doors we'd passed, rapping smartly on its dark brown surface, and then ushered me inside.

Taking a huge breath I stared at the stranger who was my boss. When I'd attended the interview I was seen by someone else, as the Accounts Manager was on holiday. I prayed hard that he liked what he saw. Unravelling his tall frame from the confines of his chair, he extended a long, slim hand towards me, dark brown eyes crinkling at the corners as his lips lifted into a smile of welcome.

Awe-struck I gazed up, realising he was at least six feet two inches, at his well-muscled, although slim, body encased in a dark brown, pin-striped suit, pristine white shirt, without a crease in sight, tie held neatly in place with a gleaming pin, and smiled as I caught a hint of Old Spice after-shave, feeling I would enjoy working with this man.

Thanking the Company Secretary for looking after me, he walked towards the door, ushering the older man out. Turning he placed his hands on my shoulders, sending a tremble through my body as the spicy aroma of his after-shave tickled my nose, and divested me of the mac, saying "I don't think you'll need this in here". My face coloured with embarrassment as one sleeve turned inside out, showing the hastily-repaired lining! Without looking at me, he deftly righted the sleeve and then, as if it was a precious fur, hung the mac carefully next to his own, very smart, fawn coloured raincoat on the wooden stand in one corner of his room.

I was duly installed in a huge office, containing thirty people, clerks, comptometer operators whose nimble fingers as they operated their machines had a mesmerising effect on me, an assistant accounts officer and two juniors, who all looked up as Mr A introduced me. I felt very proud, at the age of just fifteen and a half, to be known as the Junior Secretary, although the "junior" bit was superfluous as I was the only secretary in that department!

The office always smelled fresh and clean, as if spring was in attendance all year round. The canteen, divided into works and office sections, harboured, for me, the most delicious smells of all, especially when they served egg and chips, my most favourite meal even today. The meals were very appetising, and only cost a few pennies, but I still enjoyed one of Mother's filling dinners when I got home each night.

I had my first "romance" there, being sought out by one of the youths in the Finance Office. We sometimes arranged to meet in the Stationery Room, which was huge, containing rack upon metal rack of all kinds of office stationery. The first time he attempted to kiss me in there he found a box for me to stand on, being at least fourteen inches taller than me. Gingerly I stood on the box, leaning towards him for the promised kiss.

In my head I heard bells ringing, and thought I had fallen in love. At his hissed "Hurry up, the end of break bell has just gone", I moved too quickly, causing my stiletto heel to catch in the box which, in turn, fell, sending me crashing into his slightly bent body. Although I was very slight the unexpected lunge sent him flying backwards into one of the racks. Paper, box files, paper clips and all kinds of paraphernalia cascaded to the floor,

172

and he left me to clear it all up! Luckily no-one else was using the stationery room that day.

I enjoyed working there, although in the beginning there was a bit of jealousy from girls around my age as my position was senior to their own. However, once they realised just how nervous I was, and without any airs and graces, we all got on really well. One of the girls, who didn't actually work in the Accounts Office but in the Post Room, is a friend to this day, over thirty years later.

I have worked in many different environments since those days but the one job I remember with fondness is my brief spell with Mr J and his band of merry men. Every time I hear the stirring, haunting tune of "Men of Harlech", or catch a hint of engine oil or the elusive, sea-scented after-shave that Bernie wore, tears fill my eyes, and I wonder where they all are now.

CHAPTER
EIGHTEEN

Christmas Eve

Home-made paper chains swing gently in the air,
hiding the damp patches on the ceiling.
The tree, adorned with age-old ornaments,
and a lop-sided fairy resplendent in a piece of lace,
stands crookedly on the scratched and scarred surface
  of the chiffonier.

Dark green holly, sharp, culled from the park,
draped haphazardly over the dull mirror,
its blood red berries gleaming.
A hopeful bunch of mistletoe hangs at head height
  by the door,
but none of us know how it got there!

Wonderful smells emanating from the scullery;
the turkey, a gift to my Father, sits fatly in the
  roasting tin
surrounded by small, succulent sausages,
strips of bacon releasing their juices over the skin.
Mother's shining face, flushed from the heat,
greets me as I enter her domain.

Softly she sings "Silent Night", whilst busily peeling
  the vegetables.
Together we sing the beautiful words
while Father hums — out of tune.
Soft snow flakes descend, bringing my siblings inside
to the once-a-year warmth, and magic
of that little house.

Christmas

I love Christmas, and remember so vividly the Christmases of my childhood. At this very special time every family in the yard did their very best to have the most amazing displays in their windows. Our cotton wool balls of "snow" and shining silver stars, cut out of cigarette paper, looked every bit as good as the windows with small, twinkling electric tree lights, I thought.

Our sparse-branched tree, which started off quite healthy until we children had decorated it, held an array of silver-painted fir cones, bits of cotton wool stuck to the ends of the branches to resemble snow, a red-breasted and battered robin (obtained from Heaven knew where), sat drunkenly resplendent on the short, spiky branches, his scarred features gazing up at the "fairy" — our youngest sister's doll — draped in a piece of lace purchased from the rag market in the city, with a piece of shiny tinsel wound round her straw-like, blond hair. We always tied her to the topmost branch with a piece of string as Jean, the baby, was always crying that she wanted her dolly back!

Crêpe paper, usually red, green and bright yellow, was teased into all kinds of shapes, fans, chains and flowers then stuck on the walls with drawing pins, the remainder being festooned across the ceiling, but well away from the gas mantle! Bits of tinsel, and holly (culled from the park), its red berries gleaming in the fire's glow, were stuck at either side of the mirror on the chiffonier, helping to hide the mottled surface. A piece of mistletoe, which appeared every year but none of us knew from whence it came, hung at head-height by the kitchen door, enticing all who entered to take advantage, but no-one ever did!

For about a month before Christmas Day the entire house smelled delicious as Mother made the Christmas puddings and the Cake! I loved it when she let us run our fingers round the bowl in which the puddings were made, licking them clean of the fragrant, spicy mixture. The puddings were wrapped in a piece of clean linen, tied with string and placed inside a medium-sized saucepan, which in turn was placed into a larger saucepan, the latter filled with water. A plate acted as a lid on top of the interior saucepan, held down with a piece of brick, and the puddings bubbled away merrily for hours.

Strangers coming into the yard would sniff the air, smiles breaking out on their faces as they whispered "Ah, Christmas Pudding!". After the puddings were cooked, Mother hung them from a hook, specially made by Father for that very purpose, in the kitchen, where they dried out and matured. After four weeks of being driven mad by the smell we couldn't face eating it on Christmas Day! Mother gave some away to the Church for the elderly, which I am sure they enjoyed as they hadn't lived with the smell! The remainder were used up with custard, or cream, after our Sunday dinner for many weeks after Christmas!

The smell of the Christmas Cake she made was divine. I can still smell the gorgeous, tangy, orangey aroma as Mother patiently folded in flour, eggs, syrup, nutmeg, candied peel and raisins, the mixture growing darker and richer by the second. Our house smelled even more delicious than the bakery at Christmas, and we were loathe to leave its warmth to walk to school in biting winds, rain and snow.

On Christmas Eve Father usually brought home a fresh turkey, a gift from one of the many farmers he assisted during the year, which Mother patiently cleaned, stripping it of its feathers and removing its innards whilst sitting on the doorstep. The smell was horrendous and all the children in the yard walked around with clothes peg on their noses until she had finished the task!

Before going to Midnight Mass on Christmas Eve Father would bring out the long-awaited basket of fruit, the prize he won for playing Whist. A pineapple was the main item which Father sliced up, his hardened fingers not feeling the spikes, and hand each of us a piece. Biting into the tender, succulent fruit, juice running down our chins, we tried to ignore the tiny cuts our lips received from the prickly spikes, and the sensation of coldness in our gums, revelling instead in the wonderful, spicy scent and taste.

After Midnight Mass, sitting around the glowing fire with cups of warm cocoa clasped tightly in our hands, our parents regaled us with tales of their childhood at home in Ireland. Later we fell into bed, to dream of hobgoblins, fairies and the little people, and of course Father Christmas.

Waking on Christmas morning, having stayed awake half the night in the hope of seeing Father Christmas, our eyes would light up when we espied the bulging stocking hanging along the edge of the mantlepiece above the fireplace in the bedroom. Our parents could be heard moving around downstairs, Mother joining in the singing of Christmas carols being sung on the radio. With shouts of joy the stockings were pulled onto the bed, each contained exactly the same, an apple, orange, small bar of chocolate, a few nuts and a small toy.

Downstairs, we knew, were the real presents and I remember the Christmas I was fifteen, after praying hard to my God for many long weeks for a new coat, feeling the most awful disappointment ever to find a doll at the bottom of the tree. Although she was beautiful, dressed in a gorgeous pale pink organdie dress, beribboned dark brown hair and beautiful blue eyes, I hated her! Looking back now I should have realised the impossibility of my parents ever affording a new coat for me, or any of us really. When I made my Confession the following week, Father O'Keefe didn't chastise me, as I expected, but said in a small, sad voice "Oh Mary, my child, think how hard your parents worked in order to buy you that doll", causing me to cry copiously when he went on to say "Just think of all the children who don't receive any gifts at all!". The shame of that day stayed with me for a long time. Eventually I came to love that doll, finally giving her to my first-born when she was just a baby!

Most of the neighbours came out into the yard on Christmas morning, shouting "Merry Christmas" to everyone, their faces glowing, the Mothers from the heat of the kitchen, the Fathers from the alcohol they'd obviously consumed the night before! All the children showed off their presents, smirking if they had something really expensive, but we pretended indifference".

179

My birthday is on Boxing Day, and somehow my parents always managed to find a few extra shillings to purchase a birthday present and card for me. I think then I was more excited about my birthday than Christmas Day!

Our Christmas dinner was wonderful, the golden turkey sat proudly in a bowl, and all thoughts of the awful smell just the day before disappeared from our minds. Loads of creamy, mashed potatoes, dark green cabbage, peas, roast potatoes and lovely, Bisto, gravy shuffled for room on our plates as Father placed huge pieces of turkey alongside. The remainder of the fruit from Father's win gleamed at us from a big, oval bowl on top of the piano, its usually untidy surface having been cleared for this purpose. The enticing aroma of rice pudding seeped out from the kitchen, mingling with aroma of the Christmas meal. As soon as dinner was over, Mother turned up the radio for the Queen's Speech whilst we children shuffled restlessly in our seats. After what seemed an interminable time, tidying up, washing up, putting things away, we were released into the freedom of the yard, there to play marbles, hop-scotch (weather permitting) or to indulge in our "Talent" shows!

Loudly I sang the beautiful words of carol after carol, firmly believing that, one day, a talent scout, driving up the lane in his motor car, would be so enthralled with the sound of my voice, he'd stop to listen, and my fortune would be made! Each girl sang louder and louder until our parents bellowed at us to "Either shut up or come inside", so ending that particular bit of fun.

One Christmas Mother entered me for a Talent Show

at Bingley Hall, Father having chosen his favourite song of the time for me to sing, "The Oak and the Ash". Trembling in the wings, I wiped my sweaty hands down the sides of my second-hand, pale lemon dress, willing myself to calm down. The ringlets Mother had teased into my long, black hair, bedecked with ribbons to match the dress, drooped sadly in the heat of the lights. As the other children performed I felt quite confident that I was as good as, if not better, than most of them. When a golden-haired girl, wearing a beautiful, and obviously brand new, blue dress, hair in ringlets tied up with blue ribbon, and dainty black shiny ballet shoes on her feet, started to sing "In My Sweet Little Alice Blue Gown", I knew I didn't stand a chance. My voice was far better than hers, I thought then, but her appearance said it all.

At the end of the contest, the compère stood behind each child, holding a numbered board above our heads, and invited the audience to clap "as hard as possible". The girl in blue came first, a boy aged about four, who sang, rather badly I thought, "The Lord is My Shepherd", came second and, to my utter surprise and delight, I came third. Peering down into the darkened auditorium I espied Mother, tears running down her face, and clapping harder than anyone else, as the announcement was made. I received a whole box of chocolates for my efforts, which I kept to share out on Christmas Day. Unfortunately there weren't any "talent" scouts in the audience, but despite that, I think that was the best and most enjoyable Christmas I ever had as a child!

The girls at school didn't believe I had actually been placed, and even to this day I find it hard to believe too!

CHAPTER
NINETEEN

Goodbye

Today I left
my childhood
behind,
in your
narrow entry,
your blue
brick
yard,
your small dark
houses,
the narrow
streets,
the playgrounds,
the park,
and
I am
sad.

Demolition!

When the air raid shelter was demolished it sparked great excitement in the yard, and adults and children alike stood in awe as the men from the Council swung their huge pickaxes and hammers at the resisting brickwork. Some of us went dangerously close to their swinging arms, only to be yelled at by the men, thus sending us scurrying back to the safety of our doorsteps. The amount of rubbish they pulled out from its cavernous interior prior to its destruction was unbelievable, and we could hear the adults muttering "So that's where that went to!", surprise evident in their tone, as yet another old pram, mattress or armchair joined their companions on the steadily growing heap at the top of the entry. Suddenly a huge rat ran across the yard, eyes blinking in the unaccustomed daylight, and made its way to the centre drain. Women and children shrieked with fear, their screams turning to sighs of "Ah" when an accurately aimed shovel stopped its flight. I can still see its crushed body lying by the drain, its blood mingling with the other unsavoury paraphernalia from the shelter. Spiders, beetles and cockroaches scurried hither and thither and we closed our doors, terrified in case they made their new homes with us.

As the final barrow-load of rubbish was carted away we waited, with baited breath, for the first blow to be struck, exhaling slowly as the shelter began to crumble. I felt a bit sad as we had played many of our games on its unprotesting roof, used much of its hidden store for our bonfires as well as using its exterior walls for our chalked "works of art", washed away as soon as it rained.

Clouds of chalky dust hung on the summer air, enforcing the women to close all the windows in the small, airless houses. The pungent smell that emanated from the failing bricks was obnoxious to us all. Mother said it smelled like Death — perhaps she was right I thought for, after all, the shelter was dying. Someone else remarked it was due to the rotting wood, old clothes etc which had lain festering in its dark interior for many years. I don't know what it was, I only hope I never smell anything like it again.

The inside of our house seemed so much lighter once the shelter had finally been raised to the ground. No longer did we need the gas light flaring away all day in the kitchen, for now natural daylight crept in, almost stealthily, through the single paned window. The living room, once shadowed even in summer, now was filled with light, so bright at times we had to close the blinds!

We had lots more room to play our summer-time games and revelled in the extra space. Within just a few weeks the shelter was forgotten, as though it had existed only in our imaginations, the only reminder being the pitted and grooved bricks where it had once stood.

During the early months of 1962 some men appeared in the yard, notebooks tucked under their arms, measuring tapes stretched criss-cross under the washing lines. Mrs H commented that she had heard a rumour that Wimbush bakery wanted to buy the land to create a huge car park for their lorries. Joan remarked that her husband said it was something to do with Urban

Renewal, which we knew had been going on in other parts of the city.

We were eventually told that we were being demolished under a slum clearance schedule. I was very offended to think we had lived in a slum for sixteen years for the dictionary definition is "dirty, crowded, poor district in a town". The adults didn't care what our area was called, they were pleased to be moving to bigger and better accommodation. Once I got over the shock of being a slum-dweller, I too looked forward to living in a better house. I prayed one Sunday for a house with a bathroom and inside toilet, and of course electricity, promising my God I would be good for the rest of my life if he complied!

The women spent weeks spring-cleaning those little houses, from top to bottom, and even the brew house was given a good going over. I couldn't understand why they were being so fussy, after all the houses were going to be pulled down anyway! Mother explained that the cleaner the houses and yard looked when the "Visitor", spoken in hushed tones, descended upon us, the better chance there was of obtaining a house in a good area. I think my Mother went a bit over the top when she scrubbed the outside, upstairs windowsills, hanging out at a precarious angle with the blue cobbled bricks below just waiting for her to fall!

Suddenly, or so it seemed, the exodus began. First to leave was Joan and her little family, they were moving to Sheldon. Joan was trembling with excitement as she told the other women of the lovely little garden, the inside loo, and the plans Charlie had for building her an "outhouse". I think she meant a conservatory as she'd once shown me one in one of the many magazines she indulged in!

One good thing came out of their move, Joan gave me lots of her cast-off clothes, which were quite fashionable for someone of her age!

One by one the houses emptied of their occupants, their boarded up windows a sad reminder that our friends had left, some never to be seen again. Walking along the lane now was eerie, half of the houses had been demolished, those remaining were boarded up, concealing all the dramas of the past. Everywhere looked sad, neglected and smelled empty and I wished the Council would hurry up and move us away from this awful, silent place.

The sight of a honeysuckle climber, clinging to the remains of the wall of a house in the lane, brought a lump to my throat even as its scent filled my head with memories of the people who had lived, worked, played and loved here. Echoes of the happy, mad and some-times sad times went round and round in my head like the wheels of a train, my heart weeping silently.

I missed the friendly chatter of the women on washing days, the sneaky look through Mrs H's window at the television, the warmth of Joan's living room as I styled her hair, the talent shows and the cheeky banter of the younger children as I sauntered down the entry in my new, three inch stiletto heels! I was fast approaching my sixteenth birthday and going through a "romantic" phase where, in my heart, everything I'd known and loved was far more beautiful than the reality.

Even Nigs, our cat, was unsettled, and crept more and more often into my Father's lap, mewing loudly. As each family moved out he sat rigidly at the top of the entry, crying his farewells, returning to the comforting warmth of my Father's gentle stroking.

Throughout my working day as Junior Secretary to an Accountant, I found myself making silly errors and was called to task by my boss. He was aghast when I burst into tears, soaking the letters I held in my hands. When I told him why I felt so sad he was very understanding, and told me he felt like that when he had to leave his childhood home. His situation was worse than mine, for his Father had died when my boss was only in his teens. He went on to say that, wherever I lived in the future, I would always carry the past in my heart. Much cheered by this I decided to be more positive about something I had no power to control anyway!

Suddenly it was our turn. Like a whirlwind Mother cleaned, packed, unpacked, cried, laughed, sang and generally drove us mad with her constant demands for "Fetch this" etc. She and Father disappeared on numerous occasions to the new house to measure up for lino and curtains.

A few days before we moved I found Mother sitting on the edge of their bed, her pretty face sad. Slowly she told me of the hopes and dreams she'd harboured on the journey over from Ireland all those years ago. "Sure I believed I would find the crock of gold at the end of my rainbow, child, now isn't that silly!" she choked, gripping the window cleaning cloth, soaked in vinegar, to her nose. Her lovely blue eyes filled with tears as she whispered "Sure I've known great sadness in this house. 'twas here I heard of the deaths of my parents, and lost my little boy". My tears joined hers as I too remembered the sad times. Trying to cheer her up I stammered "But you have been happy too, haven't you?".

Wiping her eyes and grimacing as the vinegar came into contact with them, she sniffed and said "Oh, sure I have, didn't I have four beautiful daughters in this lovely city!". Her normal good humour restored we set to and finished packing the bed clothes. While we worked she told me of her arrival at the house in the lane, "Sure the floors were thick with muck and the mice were more at home here than we were!" she laughed. I learned of the months of hard work to make the house habitable and my heart filled with love as I envisaged her, fresh from the Emerald Isle and all its glory, arriving in the place which was to be her home for sixteen years.

My heart felt heavy as she described the many years it took for her to feel at home in this different world, so far from the comfort of her life back home, her friends and her total involvement in her old community. Yet remnants of her past were always with her, I thought, as I gently packed the Crucifix and the holy pictures from her childhood home. Her memories were locked deep inside her, never to be forgotten. She spoke of how strange she felt in war-weary Britain, and I realised then just how hard her life had really been, bringing up six children in a tiny house, very little money and few luxuries, yet she never complained.

Never had I admired or loved my Mother so much as

on that special day. I believe that was the day I finally grew up.

She then told me of the house we were moving to and my excitement knew no bounds. All the things I'd prayed for were coming true and I thanked my God wholeheartedly, promising I would be true to Him for the rest of my life.

The house was, at last, empty. All our belongings were now in the cavernous interior of the removal van, only awaiting our presence to start its journey. My brothers were going to the new house straight from work that evening but I had been given a day off to assist my Mother. My parents were riding up front with the driver, a position I envied, and we girls were riding in the back.

Hands hampered by various bags and string-tied parcels I walked slowly down the yard, stopping at the top of the entry for one last lingering look. Ours was the only house not yet boarded up, its naked windows obscene in the summer sun. The other houses looked sinister in their wooden coated shells, and I shivered and dragged my eyes away.

Granny Smith and Young Tom came out, both hugging me tightly, tears running down their lined faces. "Take care, Mary dear" Granny Smith smiled through her tears, "don't forget us!". Trying to stem my own tears I stepped backwards into the echoing darkness of the entry and then stopped remembering, it was here I had received my very first kiss, at the age of eleven, from a tall dark handsome boy in my last year at the junior school. I remembered the warm feelings I had towards him in those days and wondered where he was now. The sight of the scrawled "M loves R" etched in the brickwork brought a lump to my throat and I smiled, sadly, remembering the occasion.

In my head I heard childish voices as we played our summer-time games, coupled with the shouts of the adults when we got out of hand. My eyes scanned, for the last time, the four square houses awaiting the demolition gang, and I was glad I wouldn't be there to witness the final devastation. A hint of bleach hung in the air, the results of Young Tom washing down the yard that morning to allay the summer-time dust, and I hurried out of the entry and into the lane.

My last sight of the lane was a backwards view over the tailgate of the removal van. As the vehicle rumbled slowly along the uneven surface I waved to the few people who were left. Mrs L, her brood of children hanging onto her long black skirts, shouted "Tarrah, love, all the best, it's our turn next!" Tears filled my eyes as the van trundled along, past Maud's, her cat sitting forlornly on the cardinal-polished doorstep, his usual haughty figure drooping with sadness. The Cricketer's Arms, its stout doors tightly closed, almost as if it resented the fact that it alone would remain in the wilderness, brought to mind the warm, summer evenings when the customers spilled out onto the forecourt, the young men calling to us as we sauntered past.

On my right the up and over doors of Wimbush bakery glinted in the fine drizzle now falling, the delicious smells reminding me so poignantly of the years gone by. Would we ever again know such delicious aromas I wondered. The red brick walls of the swimming baths on my left looked lonely, the rain like tears washing away my past. The air around the baths was heavy with the stench of ozone and I smiled inwardly as I realised my futile attempts at swimming, and the many instances where I'd almost drowned!

There were reminders of my childhood everywhere I looked, the slaughterhouse, its stench disgusting on a summer day, the pawn shop, the library, dear old Woolies, the Blues ground and, in my imagination I believed that every one of them felt as I was feeling. The rain seemed very appropriate then.

As we drove along Coventry Road Theresa said "I wonder what the new house will be like?". Turning towards her I told her that it had electricity, three bed-rooms, attics, an inside loo and a bathroom and, wonder of wonders, a garden. Already I could feel the soft, sweet-smelling grass under my feet instead of the hard, unyielding blue bricks of the yard. Theresa's eyes widened in delight as she whispered "Will we be able to have a television, do you think?", her face breaking into smiles when I nodded.

She made me realise that life would be much better for us all, Mother wouldn't have to fight a never-ending battle with grime and bugs, my younger sisters would have plenty of room to play, the boys would have space for hobbies and I, at last, would be just like my con-temporaries! I would be able to buy the latest hit record and play it on a proper record player, invite friends to stay overnight and, perhaps, one day, a boyfriend would come calling!

Twisting fully round on the piece of sacking that

graced the bottom of the van, I smiled at my siblings, catching my breath as the delightful aroma of fresh-baked apple tarts assailed my nostrils as we passed Greenway Street, the tantalising scents ensuring I would never, ever forget Small Heath, and turned my face to the Future.

CHAPTER
TWENTY

The Return

"Don't go back", my family said
"It's always a mistake"!
I wouldn't listen to their pleas —
"This journey I must make".

The rain was falling softly
when I arrived in the lane,
sadly, so different now,
filling my soul with pain.

Inhaling deeply I tried so hard
to recapture days gone by,
tears running down my cheeks,
my heart heaving a sigh.

Net-curtained windows watched me
as I scanned the lonely scene,
bereft of everything I'd loved,
and everything I'd been.

No sounds of life filled the air
in that strange, unfriendly place,

and no matter where I looked
I saw no smiling face.

Trembling now with heartache
I turned to walk away,
when, suddenly, a familiar smell
cut through the dreary day.

Memories engulfed my being
as I sniffed the fragrant air,
seeing, so clearly now
friendly faces everywhere.

Echoes of my childhood years
filtered inside my head,
thanks to the evocative aroma
of fresh-baked, crusty bread!

CHAPTER
TWENTY-ONE

My Pilgrimage

I'm here, in the cottage where my Father was born,
unable to speak
on this lovely May morn.

For years I have longed to visit his land,
where a stranger is welcomed
with the touch of a hand.

I learned of the little folk, the cute Leprechaun,
and the wailing Banshee —
disappearing at dawn.

He told me of mountains, rivers and streams,
filling my young mind
with beautiful dreams.

Breath-taking sunsets, the vivid sunrise,
and the millions of stars
that filled the night skies.

With reverence he told of the fields of green,
and I longed for vistas
yet to be seen.

His soft, lilting voice filled me with awe
when he spoke of the history
and his country's folklore.

He promised that, some day, he'd take me there
to see all the wonders
that, together, we'd share.

My dreams, at last, are all coming true,
and as I travelled
I saw wonders anew.

Marring the pleasure in fulfilling my dream
is walking alone,
where he has been.

Now I am here, holding things he has touched,
feeling his presence,
missing him so much.

Epilogue
May 1994

On top of magnificent mountains in this rich, green land I have stood, gazing awe-struck at incredible views, held my breath as hang-gliders stepped into space, then swooped into the air, at one with the birds, the deep blue sky and the mountain peaks, my heart soaring with them.

Beauty is all around me; from the leaping salmon in the mighty Shannon, the towering Black mountain, the wonderful grottoes dotted all around the countryside, and even the haunting loneliness of Vinegar Hill, its stone lookout bereft, yet full of history.

Love overcame me as I knelt, for the very first time, at the graves of three generations of my ancestors under the shade of yew trees in the ancient country cemetery. Tears rained down my face when I touched the granite, lichen-covered headstone depicting the names of relatives I never knew. For many minutes I knelt there, praying to my God that all beneath me were safe in His arms.

Now I have reached the place I have dreamed of all my life. The cottage, built of rough-hewn stone by my Great-great-great Grandfather, stands small and mellow in the late morning sun, its four, tiny-paned windows smiling at me, the green painted centre door slightly ajar, beckoning.

Unlatching the hook on the black iron gate I feel a sense of *déjà-vu* as I step onto the well-worn, cobbled, path, envisaging the pounding feet of generations long gone. The scent of lilac, blossom and burning peat assail

197

me and I feel giddy as I approach the shadowy figure standing by the door, flat cap pulled well down over his brow, check jacket, too short in the sleeves, covering slightly stooped shoulders.

Uncle Pat, my Father's youngest brother, stands un-moving, tears raining down his weather-beaten face. In his blue eyes I see the shadow of the person who should have shared this pilgrimage with me — my Father. To walk, to fish, to climb the mountains with him whilst he talked of his youth — but it was not to be. Yet, as I smile tearfully and step into my Uncle's welcoming embrace, I feel my Father's presence all around me, and my heart, at last at peace.

ISIS publish a wide range of books in large print, from fiction to biography. A full list of titles is available free of charge from the address below. Alternatively, contact your local library for details of their collection of ISIS large print books.

Details of ISIS complete and unabridged audio books are also available.

Any suggestions for books you would like to see in large print or audio are always welcome.

7 Centremead
Osney Mead
Oxford OX2 0ES
(01865) 250333

ISIS REMINISCENCE SERIES

The ISIS Reminiscence Series has been developed with the older reader in mind. Well-loved in their own right, these titles have been chosen for their memory-evoking content.

FRED ARCHER
The Cuckoo Pen
The Distant Scene
The Village Doctor

BRENDA BULLOCK
A Pocket With A Hole

WILLIAM COOPER
From Early Life

KATHLEEN DAYUS
All My Days
The Best of Times
Her People

DENIS FARRIER
Country Vet

WINIFRED FOLEY
Back to the Forest
No Pipe Dreams for Father

PEGGY GRAYSON
Buttercup Jill

JACK HARGREAVES
The Old Country

ISIS REMINISCENCE SERIES

ISIS REMINISCENCE SERIES

BIOGRAPHY & AUTOBIOGRAPHY

NINA BAWDEN
In My Own Time

SALLY BECKER
The Angel of Mostar

CHRISTABEL BIELENBERG
The Road Ahead

CAROLINE BLACKWOOD
The Last of the Duchess

ALAN BLOOM
Come You Here, Boy!

ADRIENNE BLUE
Martina Unauthorized

BARBARA CARTLAND
I Reach for the Stars

CATRINE CLAY
Princess to Queen

JILL KERR CONWAY
True North

DAVID DAY
The Bevin Boy

MARGARET DURRELL
Whatever Happened to Margo?

BIOGRAPHY & AUTOBIOGRAPHY

MONICA EDWARDS
The Unsought Farm
The Cats of Punchbowl Farm

CHRISTOPHER FALKUS
The Life and Times of Charles II

LADY FORTESCUE
Sunset House

EUGENIE FRASER
The Dvina Remains
The House By the Dvina

KIT FRASER
Toff Down Pit

KENNETH HARRIS
The Queen

DON HAWORTH
The Fred Dibnah Story

PAUL HEINEY
Pulling Punches
Second Crop

SARA HENDERSON
From Strength to Strength

PAUL JAMES
Princess Alexandra

BIOGRAPHY & AUTOBIOGRAPHY

EILEEN JONES
Neil Kinnock

JAMES LEITH
Ironing John

FLAVIA LENG
Daphne du Maurier

MARGARET LEWIS
Edith Pargeter: Ellis Peters

VICTORIA MASSEY
One Child's War

NORMAN MURSELL
Come Dawn, Come Dusk

MICHAEL NICHOLSON
Natasha's Story

LESLEY O'BRIEN
Mary MacKillop Unveiled

ADRIAN PLASS
The Sacred Diary of Adrian Plass Aged 37 ³/₄

CHRIS RYAN
The One That Got Away

J. OSWALD SANDERS
Enjoying Your Best Years

VERNON SCANNELL
Drums of Morning

BIOGRAPHY & AUTOBIOGRAPHY

STEPHANIE SLATER WITH PAT LANCASTER
Beyond Fear

DAVA SOBEL
Longitude

DOUGLAS SUTHERLAND
Against the Wind
Born Yesterday

ALICE TAYLOR
The Night Before Christmas

SOPHIE THURNHAM
Sophie's Journey

CHRISTOPHER WILSON
A Greater Love

GENERAL NON-FICTION

RICHARD, EARL OF BRADFORD
Stately Secrets

WILLIAM CASH
Educating William

CLIVE DUNN
Permission to Laugh

EMMA FORD
Countrywomen

LADY FORTESCUE
Sunset House

JOANNA GOLDSWORTHY
Mothers: Reflections by Daughters

PATRICIA GREEN, CHARLES COLLINGWOOD
& HEIDI NIKLAUS
The Book of The Archers

HELENE HANFF
Letter From New York

ANDREW & MARIA HUBERT
A Wartime Christmas

MARGARET HUMPHREYS
Empty Cradles

JAMES LEITH
Ironing John

LESLEY LEWIS
The Private Life Of A Country House

GENERAL NON-FICTION

PETER MARREN & MIKE BIRKHEAD
Postcards From the Country

DESMOND MORRIS
The Human Animal

PHYLLIS NICHOLSON
Country Bouquet

FRANK PEARCE
Heroes of the Fourth Service

DAVA SOBEL
Longitude

SHEILA STEWART
Ramlin Rose

JOANNA TROLLOPE
Britannia's Daughters

NICHOLAS WITCHELL
The Loch Ness Story

ANIMALS

DAVID ATTENBOROUGH
Zoo Quest to Guyana

ALAN COREN
Animal Passions

MONICA EDWARDS
The Cats of Punchbowl Farm

PAUL HEINEY
Pulling Punches
Second Crop

PETER IRESON
Guiding Stars

SARAH KENNEDY
Terrible Pets

GLENDA SPOONER
For Love of Horses

ELISABETH SVENDSEN
Down Among the Donkeys
For the Love of Donkeys

ELIZABETH MARSHALL THOMAS
The Tribe of Tiger

GARDENS & PLANTS

DAVID ATTENBOROUGH
The Private Life of Plants

ALAN BLOOM
Come You Here, Boy!

RICHARD BRIERS
A Little Light Weeding

CHRISTOPHER LLOYD
In My Garden

JEAN STONE & LOUISE BRODIE
Tales of the Old Gardeners